Dearest Dawid

May Hashem
ya prayers

Much love
Shaul

MEAN
what you
PRAY

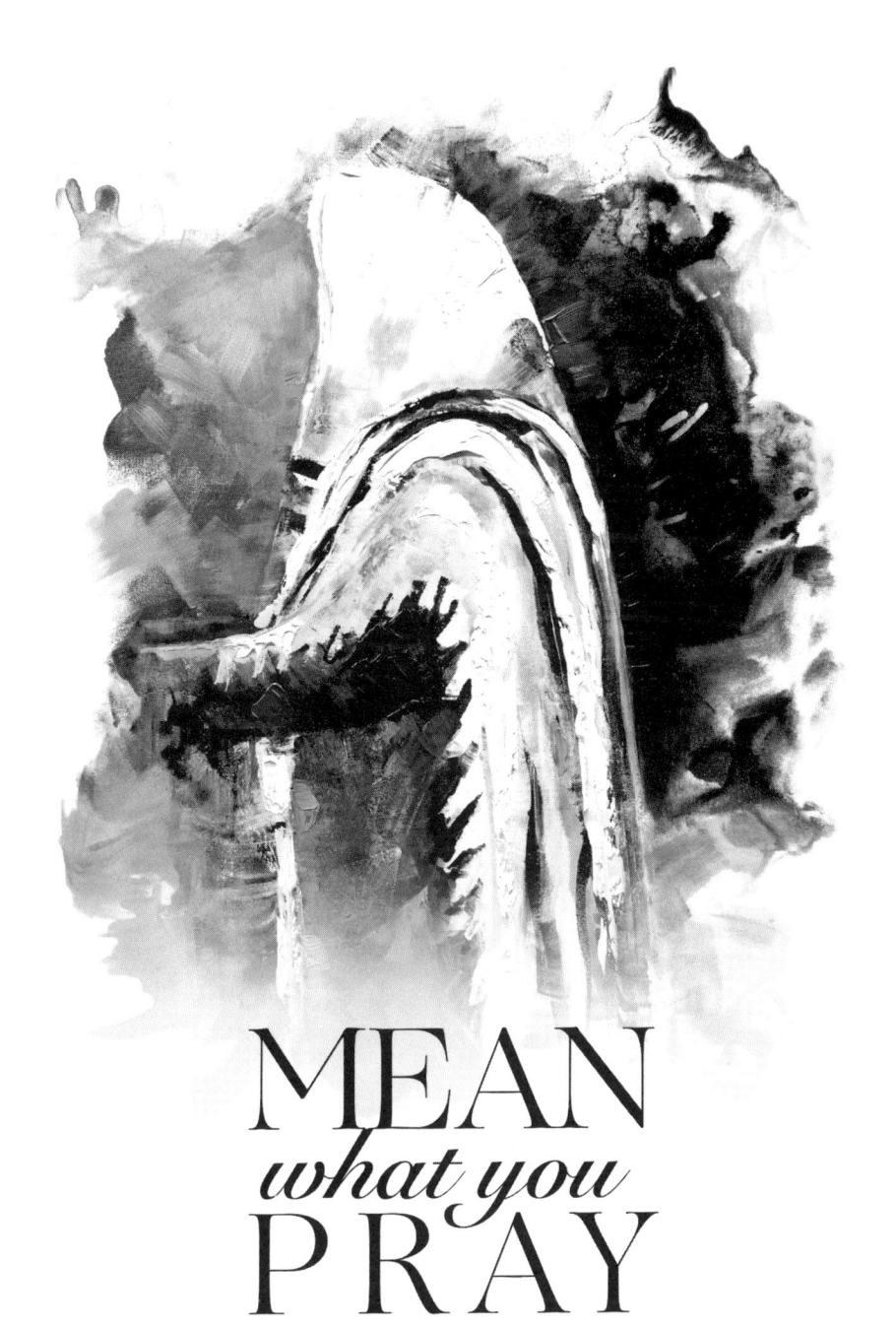

A PRACTICAL GUIDE TO CONNECTING IN PRAYER

RABBI SHAUL ROSENBLATT

Mean What You Pray
A practical guide to connecting in prayer

Rabbi Shaul Rosenblatt

Copyright © April 2022 / Iyar 5782:
Rabbi Shaul Rosenblatt.
All rights reserved.

ISBN: 978-1-988022-76-5

Front cover art by Osnat Tzadok
www.OsnatFineArt.com

Tikun was founded in 2005 by Rabbi Shaul Rosenblatt, to provide meaningful Jewish education at all levels. Its approach is based on the hashkofos of his Rebbe, R Noach Weinberg *Ztz"l*, who used to teach that Torah's full name is Toras Chaim. Torah should be viewed as 'instructions for life', he would say. Tikun takes its cue from him and aims to present Torah in a way that points very practically towards a deeper and more tangible relationship with Hashem.

To discuss publishing your material — self-publishing or regular publishing — email: *submissions@AdirPress.com* or visit us at *www.AdirPress.com*

No part of this publication may be translated, reproduced, stored in a retrieval system or transmitted in any form or by any means; electronic, mechanical, photocopying, recording or otherwise without prior permission from the copyright holder — except for a reviewer wishing to quote brief passages in connection with a review for inclusion in a magazine or newspaper.

aish HaTorah

— ישיבת —
אש התורה

בס"ד ירושלים ח"י סיון בשנ"ר תשפ"א

I have read much of Rabbi Shaul Rosenblatt's latest book *Mean What You Pray* and just cannot wait to see it published. Prayer is the most obvious way to connect with The Creator, and His availability to listen to our prayers wherever we may be is referred to in the Torah as something unique and special. To our dismay, the widespread lack of understanding of what prayer is, has made way for so many to view it as a burdensome, meaningless ritual that is practiced as a matter of tradition. In reality, one who regularly prays in a meaningful way learns to deal with both the beautiful moments as well as the challenges of life with deepfelt positive emotion.

This book restores the awareness of prayer as speaking with The Almighty, and clarifies just why this is so important. It shows how the siddur not only provides for us a text for expressing our feelings towards HaSHem, but also sets for the Jew a clear sense of priorities, what precisely is important enough to request of The Creator.

Rabbi Rosenblatt is one who lives with a deep sense of G-d awareness and is by all means the appropriate advocate for meaningful prayer. I am sure that all who study this book will find themselves speaking to The Creator in a very real and intelligent manner.

May the author continute to provide educational programs and material for all of our brethren with his clarity, wisdom and sincerity.

בברכה,
יצחק ברקוביץ

מייסד
הרב נח וינברג זצ"ל

ראש הישיבה
הרב יצחק ברקוביץ

מנכ"ל
הרב סניב בורג

מנהל
הרב דוד ראסמן

מרכז עולמי
ע"ש משפחת דן קנדה

סניפים:
קליפטון - ניו ג'רזי
אש קמפוס
מנצ'סטר
מלבורן-אוסטרליה
מיניאפוליס
פרוייקט חזון
פרוייקט אינגלייר
בוסטון
בואנוס איירס
קליבלנד
קוסטה ריקה
דנור
דטרויט
הסבוה - פלושפט
יוהנסבורג
לונדון
לוס אנג'לס
מקסיקו סיטי
ניו יורק
פילדלפיה
סאו פאולו - ברזיל
תל אביב
טורונטו
וושינגטון
סט לואיס
פלורידה
צ'ילה
סן דייגו

YESHIVAT AISH HATORAH | (ע"ר) ישיבת אש התורה

עמותה רשומה:58-001-436-3 | רחבת הכותל המערבי 1 | ת.ד. 14149, הרובע היהודי 9114101, העיר העתיקה ירושלים
Registered Association No: 58-001-436-3 | One Western Wall Plaza | POB 14149, Old City 9114101, Jerusalem, Israel

www.aishglobal.com | Jerusalem@aish.com | מייל: (02) 627-3172 | פקס: (02) 628-5666 :טל

This book presents a thought-provoking guide to prayer. It strikes a mature balance between the conceptual and practical dimensions of prayer, in an easily readable format. I personally benefited from its ideas, explained by an author who clearly knows what he is talking about. Highly recommended for those who wish to take prayer seriously.

Rabbi Dr. Akiva Tatz

Dedication

This book is dedicated to my father of blessed memory, Max Rosenblatt.

Dad, you weathered the depression, landed on D-Day, fought through France, Belgium, Holland, and Germany, liberating Bergen Belsen along the way, built a business empire, lost it all, then got back on your feet and provided for your family and so many others. You are my inspiration, my role model, and my hero. Along with mum, you sacrificed so much to give me the life that I have, and my gratitude to you is from the very depths of my heart.

Acknowledgments

There are always too many people to thank, and a list can never be complete. However, let me make a start. To my publisher, Moishe Kormornick of Adir Press, thank you for your input, support, and belief. We have got there in the end!

To Irwin Weiler, a true friend, such as you are, is a rarity in life. Thank you for being behind me in this project – as you are in all that I do.

To my Rebbe, Rav Noach Weinberg, ztz"l. So much of what I have learned about tefillah has been from you. In truth, this is your book, not mine. Thank you for making me who I am.

To my dear wife, Chana. Without you, I am nothing and would achieve nothing. This book is your accomplishment as much as it is mine.

To my gorgeous Jewish Nation. It is a privilege beyond measure to be a very small cog. I hope and pray that this book might provide some small measure of assistance for many of you to find a deeper and more meaningful connection with our loving Father in Heaven.

And, of course, to Hashem. This book is about how to serve You. I have tried to write it honestly, humbly, and in Your service. Thank You for the opportunity to make my own tiny contribution in this great Universe of Yours.

Publisher's Preface

The Gemara reveals that prayer is a prime example of something that is exceptionally lofty but vastly underappreciated.[1] The importance of prayer, therefore, cannot be overstated. In fact, the Kuzari writes that our thrice-daily prayer should be the main focus of our entire day with the rest of our time merely leading up to the next time we pray![2]

The benefit that we receive from praying is also something that is crucial to appreciate. The Ramchal[3] explains that Hashem constantly desires to give to His creations, therefore, He instituted daily prayer *in order* to provide us with the opportunity to receive His blessings. Specifically, this is achieved through sincere prayer which connects us to the Source of blessing in a way that a pipe slips into its socket allowing water to flow freely from the source to where it is needed. So too, when we connect to Hashem through prayer, we are connecting the channel between us and the Almighty, facilitating blessings to flow from its Source to wherever it is needed in our lives.

It is an enormous privilege to publish another book from Rabbi Shaul Rosenblatt — someone who is so

---

1. *Brachos* 6b with *Rashi*.
2. *Kuzari* 3:5.
3. *Derech Hashem* 4:5:1.

dedicated to educating Hashem's children, motivating them with his honest approach to life and engaging them with his sincerity and genuine desire to better their lives. This book is just one example of his dedication and hard work. A further illustration of Rabbi Rosenblatt's drive to enhance others' lives in any area they may need is found in the note he wrote at the end of this book:

"If there is interest in a follow-up book that talks in more detail about the other brachos in the Shemoneh Esrei, as well as those in the Shabbos and Festival Shemoneh Esrei also, I will gladly write one. Please email me at meanwhatyoupray@tikun.co.uk and if I receive ten responses, I will be happy to write part two."

It is hard to believe that anyone reading this book will *not* get in touch and insist that Rabbi Rosenblatt fulfills his promise. Having personally worked on this unique work, I certainly will be the first to send that email!

My fervent prayer is that Hashem blesses this book with incredible success, and that the reader takes these original ideas and develops them into their own means of communicating with Hashem.

B'ezras Hashem, we will all come to appreciate prayer for what it is, make it the focus of our day, and develop our relationships with the Source of all blessings.

Rabbi Moshe Kormornick
Adir Press

Contents

Dedication 5
Acknowledgments 7
Publisher's Preface 9

Introduction 13
Chapter 1. Service within the Heart 18
Chapter 2. Connecting to the Power of Prayer 41
Chapter 3. Modes of Prayer 60
Chapter 4. Shemoneh Esrei 79
Conclusion for the Reader 145

Appendix. Conceptual Shemoneh Esrei 146
Glossary 151

Introduction

The Shelah says that there are two types of people when it comes to prayer.[1] There are those who genuinely proclaim Hashem's oneness in Shema, pray to Him in *Shemoneh Esrei*, and bless His Name in the blessings. Then there are those who recite Shema but do not proclaim His oneness; they *say Shemoneh Esrei* but they are not *praying*; they *say* a blessing but they do not *bless* Him.

The Shelah adds that after looking around, he noticed that the first group of people is very, very small. Conversely, the second group is very, very large. He ends with a prayer for himself, "Please let it be that I am one of the first group and not one of the second."

For many of us, feeling a real connection with prayer is a challenge. This is unfortunate as there is so much depth and relevance available in prayer that is not being accessed by the majority of the population.

This book is written for those who wish to be in the Shelah's first group of people, who pray and mean it. If you have read this far, likely that is you. My goal is that this book will help its readers to feel connected to Hashem and

---

1. *Tamid, Ner Mitzvah* 21, quoting *Derech Chaim.*

Introduction

genuinely mean what they say when they pray *Shemoneh Esrei*. I pray that Hashem gives me the insight and understanding to be of assistance to His children in connecting to Him more deeply.

✻ ✻ ✻

The *Yalkut Shimoni* says, "Anyone who increases prayers will be answered."[2] *Chazal* do not say that he "is likely to be answered," they say he "will be answered" — a guarantee — and a guarantee from *Chazal* is not to be taken lightly. If a person prays in the appropriate manner and enough, Hashem is certain to respond.

A great example of this is a story about the great King Chizkiyahu.[3] He had refused to marry because, through Divine inspiration, he knew that he would father a child (Menasheh) who would be an evil king. The prophet Yeshayahu came to him and told him that Hashem had decreed for him to die as a result of his refusal to marry. Chizkiyahu immediately repented and asked Yeshayahu if he could marry his daughter. Yeshayahu refused, saying that Hashem had already made His mind up.

Chizkiyahu responded, "Son of Amotz, finish your prophecy and go home. I have a tradition from my ancestors that even if a sharp sword is at your neck, it is never too late to pray for mercy."

Chizkiyahu turned to the wall and prayed. Yeshayahu had hardly gotten out the door when Hashem came to him

---

2. *Shmuel* 1:1
3. *Brachos* 10a

— INTRODUCTION —

telling him to return to Chizkiyahu to tell him that he had been forgiven.

Such is the power of sincere prayer.

Another great example is found in *Gemara Taanis*.[4]

There was a famine in Eretz Yisrael and the Jewish people came to one of the great Rabbis of the time, Choni HaMe'agel, to ask him to pray for rain. He told them to bring in their Pesach ovens so they would not get wet, the equivalent of saying, "If you take me seriously, then get your umbrellas out before I start."

Choni prayed . . .

And, quite surprisingly after all the buildup, nothing happened.

So, Choni drew a circle in the sand and stepped inside. "Almighty," he cried out, "Your children have come to me in their time of need because they know that I am close to You. I swear by Your great Name that I will not step out of this circle until You answer Your children."

Immediately, it began to rain gently.

But Choni was not satisfied. "This is not the rain that I asked for," he said. "I want rain that will fill the cisterns and the wells."

The gentle rain suddenly became a deluge.

"This is also not what I asked for," Choni said. "I want rain that is a blessing, not a curse."

It began to rain strongly enough to fill the cisterns and wells, but not strongly enough to cause flooding. And it continued to rain until the Jewish people were forced to return to Choni and ask him to pray for the rain to stop.[5]

---

4. 19b
5. Ibid. 19a

— INTRODUCTION —

How incredible is the power of prayer; it can shape the world. As the *Yalkut Shimoni* says, Hashem listens to and answers the prayers of those who know how to call to Him and do so. Choni HaMe'agel was such a person.

We can all be such people. Becoming such people requires first, that we understand how to pray, and second, once we understand prayer, that we use it with all our hearts.

The purpose of this book is to help its readers fulfill the first requirement. The second is in the hands of each and every one of us: once we understand how to pray, we must open our hearts fully and know that the power that we yield is greater than that of any president, prime minister, or billionaire. With a single sincere prayer we can literally change the world.

This power is waiting for any and every one of us to command.

Almost everyone prays at some time in their life.

My teacher, Rabbi Noach Weinberg, used to ask "irreligious" people if they had ever prayed. Eighty percent told him that they had. He then asked those 80 percent whether Hashem had ever answered their prayers, and another 80 percent of those questioned responded that He had. This illustrates something of deep significance. Most human beings know there is a God and know that they can talk to Him. And most of them also know that He answers them. Prayer may not always be a part of people's lives, but when surrounded by ruthless enemies, out of ammunition and with nowhere to run, it is hard to believe that there is a single person with a heart so hard that he will not pray. When people are desperate and have nothing to lose, they will give it a go. As the saying goes, there are no atheists in a foxhole.

— INTRODUCTION —

Not only do we turn to prayer in times of need, but we also usually know just how to pray — even if we have never prayed properly before in our lives. We have a natural emotional eloquence when we are in trouble.

Unfortunately, when things are not quite so desperate, prayer becomes less attractive and more challenging, and it is often harder to know what exactly to say.

This book aims to make prayer more accessible for those who are challenged by it, and for those who are not, to increase their ability to access the power of prayer.

My goal is not only to provide an explanation of the prayers that we say — though that is certainly a part of the book. My goal is to try to explain how to go about praying in a practical way so that anyone can stand before Hashem and speak with a level of clarity and confidence. The closer our prayers can be to those of Choni HaMe'agel[6] and Chizkiyahu, the more likely they will elicit the response that these two great men received.[7]

---

6. Choni HaMe'agel referred to himself as a *"ben bayis"* before Hashem. The term *ben bayis* refers to someone who is not a member of a family but nevertheless virtually lives in their home and is looked upon as family. Choni, it would appear, "lived" in Hashem's "home," i.e., he prayed a great deal. Hence, the Jewish people came to him in their hour of need because they knew that he was the person who could elicit Hashem's mercy.

7. It should be noted that in the case of Choni, he was sternly rebuked by Rebbi Shimon ben Shatach for the seemingly disrespectful manner in which he addressed Hashem. This does not take away from the fact that the power of his prayer, though it might have been said more respectfully, was the power to command nature.

Chapter 1

Service within the Heart

The Rabbis describe prayer as *avodah shebalev* — literally "service that is within the heart."[8]

It is not *avodah shel halev* — service "of" the heart, but *shebalev* — "within" the heart.

This is a key distinction. The Gemara tells us that "Hashem wants the heart."[9] This means that every act of developing our relationship with Hashem requires that we involve the heart, be it intent when doing a mitzvah, awareness of His presence while learning Torah, or curtailment of certain desires and development of others. If we are to serve Hashem properly, then we are always looking to give Him our hearts.

If so, what is unique about prayer that it is "service within the heart"? Is not all service of Hashem heart related?

---

8. *Taanis* 2a
9. *Sanhedrin* 106b

Prayer is something unique in the service of Hashem. All service is "of" the heart; prayer, however, is the only service that is "within" the heart.

Let me explain what I mean by this in a slightly different way:

The 613 mitzvos are all modes of relating to Hashem. While most of them are expressed externally as well as internally, the mode of prayer is purely internal. The essence of the service is purely within the heart.[10]

Let's take keeping kosher as an example of a mitzvah that is not purely "in the heart." For someone who is struggling with kashrus, the desire to eat in McDonald's, for example, begins as a struggle, or service, within the heart. His strong animal instinct to eat the bacon cheeseburger competes with his mind and soul telling him that to go against the will of the Creator of this universe makes no sense at all. Yes, this is a struggle of the heart. Ultimately, however, the decision will play itself out in action. Whether or not he will eat the non-kosher food is what's relevant. The outcome is tangible, and it is easy to evaluate failure and success.

Prayer, however, is not so black and white.

The challenge and struggle of prayer is not whether to stand up and say some words or not. To read or not to read is not the question. The challenge of prayer is actually to be or not to be, to feel or not to feel. Prayer requires that we consciously experience what we are saying to Hashem. It is internal and existential. When I pray, it is not about expressing myself to Hashem with *words*. It is about expressing myself to Hashem with *feeling*. Words are merely the medium through which I do so.

---

10. Yes, it is not purely in the heart. It needs to be expressed in words, and those words need to be audible to oneself. But it is the feeling that the words express that is the essence of prayer, not the words themselves.

— CHAPTER 1 —

So when it comes to eating kosher or not, I have fulfilled Hashem's will when I walk away from McDonald's empty-handed — regardless of what I may feel. Prayer, however, is the opposite. I have done Hashem's will (i.e., the mitzvah of prayer) when I mean whatever I may say.[11] It is for this reason that Hashem did not give specific prayers for us to say.[12]

Let me put this one more way. Essentially, there are potentially three aspects that make up a mitzvah:

1. The intent that the purpose of the action we are doing is to serve Hashem (i.e., a mitzvah),
2. The act of the mitzvah itself, and
3. The understanding and focus on the meaning of the mitzvah.

Regarding the first criterion of intent, there is a debate among the Rabbis as to whether mitzvos require intent to serve Hashem, and the *Shulchan Aruch* concludes that they do.[13]

---

11. Although the *Shulchan Aruch*, O.C. 98:1 clearly defines *kavanah* as understanding the words and that one is speaking to Hashem, the Rambam (*Hilchos Tefillah* 4:16) gives a lesser definition as a minimal level, without which you have not prayed: that one knows he is standing before Hashem. In other words, one does not need intent for the words, one needs to be aware of Hashem's presence and intend the words in His direction (so to speak) even if he doesn't actually mean each word itself.

12. In other words, if prayer is about meaning what I say, it would follow logically that I have to pray for things that matter to me. Personally, if I were told to pray, for example, that I have beautiful fingernails, I would have a very hard time meaning the prayer when I said it. There may be people, however, who could say such a prayer and very much mean it. Each human being is unique, and hence Hashem left it up to each person to formulate prayers that mean something to him or to her. Nonetheless, around 2,500 years ago, the Anshei Knesses HaGedolah saw fit to formulate our prayers for us in the siddur that we pray from today. Why they did so is something that will be addressed later in the book.

13. *Orach Chaim* 60:4. In fact, going further, the Gemara (Kiddushin 40a) tells us that an intent to do a mitzvah that does not work out is still a mitzvah, thus

However, the understanding and focus on the meaning of the mitzvah, which is the third point that I mentioned above, is not a requirement in fulfilling the mitzvah itself. As long as I intend as I enter or sit in the sukkah, for example, to do Hashem's will through this action, I fulfill the mitzvah on its basic level — even if I have no idea of the meaning and purpose of the sukkah and all I am thinking about is the ice cream I am guzzling while sitting there.

This is true for all mitzvos except prayer. When it comes to prayer, the intent of the heart is primary. The actions and words that go with it are only the medium — the tangible expression of the feeling. Intent is not merely a part of prayer, it is prayer itself. To say the words of a deep and beautiful prayer while imagining oneself sipping a martini on a beach in Barbados is not simply "prayer without intent," it is not prayer at all!

Prayer is the *only* mitzvah about which the fundamental halachah tells us if one will be unable to have *kavanah*, he should simply not do it. In fact, the Rambam's language is even stronger: he says that it is *forbidden* to pray *Shemoneh Esrei* if one knows that he will not be able to concentrate on his prayer.[14] He cites an example from the Gemara of a person who returns from traveling (which was a traumatic experience in previous generations); he should not pray for three days to give his mind time to settle. Even though this is not the practical halachah today — and so, we must still pray even when we fear that we will not have sufficient *kavanah*[15] — nevertheless, it does not take away from the fact that the essence of prayer remains *kavanah*.

---

suggesting that the intent is the essence of the mitzvah itself.

14. *Hilchos Tefillah* 4:15

15. The Tur in the name of Rav Meir M'Rottenberg (*Aruch Chaim* 98:2) explains that this leniency is the result of our lack of proficiency at focusing during prayer

— CHAPTER 1 —

Prayer, in essence, is giving our hearts to Hashem. The ultimate goal is not that we get our prayers answered. In fact, in order to get us to pray, Hashem *gives us* needs. The goal of prayer is for us to experience Hashem in a very deep and passionate way, to relate to Him and connect to Him by means of a direct engagement within our hearts.[16]

As such, prayer done properly is not easy. It requires complete focus of one's consciousness.

But, on the flip side, prayer done properly can lift us into a connection to Hashem that no other mitzvah can.

True, the six constant mitzvos[17] are a more direct route to a relationship with Hashem than prayer.[18] But putting those mitzvos aside, out of the remaining 607 mitzvos given to the Jewish people, prayer is the one that calls upon us most directly to turn our hearts toward Hashem. And turning our hearts toward Hashem requires planning, effort, and ongoing focus.

I hope, through the course of these pages, to guide you to a very practical understanding of how to personalize

---

in general. If not for this, prayer would likely be forgotten from the Jewish people, since rarely would a person be able to concentrate sufficiently throughout his entire prayer in those days — all the more so for us today!

16. In truth, closeness to Hashem is the goal of *every* mitzvah, as the Ramchal says (*Mesilas Yesharim*, chap. 1), "A person should struggle to connect to Hashem through the actions whose result is that connection — and they are the mitzvos." The Maharal says (*Tiferes v'Eretz Yisrael* 9), "A man should acquire the ultimate success — connection to Hashem — and the way to come to this success is by the keeping of Torah. However, whereas other mitzvos are specific actions that bring a person closer to Hashem when he does them, prayer is different. The mitzvah *itself* is the closeness to Hashem."

17. The *Biur Halachah* quotes from the *Sefer HaChinuch* that there are six mitzvos that are purely spiritual in nature and are incumbent upon each of us every moment of every day. They are: knowing there is a God, not believing in any other power, knowing that Hashem is one, loving Him, fearing Him, and not following one's heart and eyes (1:1).

18. Loving Hashem, for example, *is* relationship, whereas prayer is an attempt to connect.

your prayers so that they will lift you into a powerful experience of connection to Hashem in day-to-day prayer and, ultimately, as those experiences build, to develop a deep and powerful relationship with Hashem, which is the ultimate purpose of Hashem's creation.[19]

Why Does Hashem Need Us to Pray?

There is an obvious first question that must be asked with regards to prayer. If Hashem is omniscient, then He surely knows what we want. And if He knows what we want, why do we need to ask Him for it?

The question is actually even stronger. Not only does Hashem know what we *want*, He knows what is best for us — what we *need*. And the two are often not the same.

A person might want to win 10 million dollars in the lottery. But how many lottery winners have found that the money has been more a curse than a blessing? They don't know who their friends are anymore. Their family suddenly has all sorts of financial expectations. Or they start to live way above their means, only to find the money goes quickly and they are left with less than they started with.

Another example might be someone who desperately wants to marry a certain person, but in reality, if he was to marry this woman he would soon realize that he had been infatuated and not seen her for who she truly is.

Someone once quipped, "Be very careful what you pray for because Hashem might just give it to you!" So yes, it is natural for us to pray for what we want — because what we

---

[19]. As the *Mesilas Yesharim* says, "Man was created *only* to rejoice in Hashem and derive pleasure in the splendor of His Presence."

CHAPTER 1

want looks like what's best for us. But wouldn't we be better off leaving that to Hashem? Consider for a moment: What would you rather end up happening — what you think is best for you or what Hashem *knows* is best for you?

With this in mind, perhaps our prayers should simply be, "Master of the universe, You know me better than I know myself. Please give me what I need in life and don't worry about what I might want." Or even better, perhaps we should say, "Master of the universe, You know me better than I know myself. It would be incredibly arrogant of me to ask You for what I want — so I will not. I recognize that You always have my best interests at heart, and I know that You will always do as you see fit. So, I just wanted to say thank You for everything that you do."

But this is not how the Anshei Knesses HaGedolah (Men of the Great Assembly) arranged our prayers. We ask for specifics like health, wisdom, and wealth.

There are many, many examples of prayer both in the Written and Oral Torah. And in every one, the supplicant was asking Hashem for a specific outcome. When Moshe prayed for Miriam to be healed, when Avraham prayed for the people of Sodom to be saved, and when Yitzchak and Rivkah prayed to be blessed with a child are but a few of the more famous examples.

The Jewish concept of prayer is to request something specific — in spite of the fact that Hashem knows what we want and what we need even better than we know ourselves.[20] (See the footnote below, where I explain further

---

20. There are, however, sources that seem to contradict this. One example is found in *Sefer HaIkarim, maamar* 4, *perek* 24: "This is the ideal prayer: 'Master of the universe, do Your will in the heavens above and give comfort to those who fear You below. And do that which is good in Your eyes.'" The author, Rav Yosef Albo, continues to say that as a result of this, one should not request specifics from Hashem, nor should one tell Hashem the details of how to give them to

that while one should ask for something specific, he should do so with the proviso and understanding that Hashem knows what is best for him, and he will therefore accept whatever outcome Hashem chooses.)

There is a simple reason for this: Hashem created this world for us to exercise our free will. He gave us an imperfect world (a *very* imperfect world, actually) and made us His partners, so to speak, in improving it. As such, we are tasked with actively taking responsibility for His world, not simply leaving Him to run it by Himself. Of course, there is a balance to be had between our own efforts and trusting in Hashem. But, wherever that balance might lie, our own efforts are very much a part of what is expected from us in this world, and in order to put in our own efforts, we must have our own opinions about what needs to be done. What is the difference, after all, between asking Hashem that he let me marry a specific girl and proposing to her? Either way, I am having an opinion as to whom I should marry and actively following through on that opinion.

And so, our job here is to have (humbly of course) opinions about how to improve our lives and the world in which we live and to actively work toward improving both. Part of those active efforts is the medium of prayer. To pray for Hashem to do what is best is like owning a field and waiting for Hashem to make something grow. Albeit that it makes

---

him. However, a careful reading of this chapter indicates that Rav Yosef Albo is warning against arrogance in prayer — which is certainly a concern to be careful about. A person does not want to think that he or she knows better than Hashem. As Rav Yosef Albo says, a person may want a child, but Hashem knows that the child, as with King David's son Avshalom, would try to kill him. Or, he may pray for wealth, but Hashem knows that wealth would lead him to an early death or denial of Hashem. So, the correct balance is to ask Hashem for what we want but also to have the humility to say to Hashem at the same time, "Do Your will, and I will accept whatever that might be."

sense, given that Hashem controls everything, it is not the way He has set this world up.

Having answered the question of why we pray for specific outcomes instead of leaving everything to Hashem to take care of, let us return to the original question: What is the purpose of prayer itself?

Let me start by stating the obvious — so obvious, in fact, that its significance is often overlooked.

There is nothing, absolutely nothing, that we can do for Hashem. None of the mitzvos that we do could possibly, in any way, add any value to an Infinite Being. He *is* everything, so he *has* everything. And if He needs nothing, then we cannot give Him anything. We are His creations; all we have is His already. As the Mishnah tells us, "Give to Him from that which is His, for you and all that is yours are His."[21]

So, being that nothing we do can possibly be of any benefit to Him, it stands to reason that everything that He wants us to do can only be for us.

It is probably easiest to appreciate this in the parent-child metaphor that the Torah often uses when discussing our relationship with Hashem. In the same way that parents insist that their children say please and thank you — for their own ultimate benefit — so Hashem insists that we act in certain ways — for our own ultimate benefit.

So, although our prayers are directed at Hashem, their benefits are directed at us. Prayer is like a giant magnifying mirror. The more we pour in Hashem's direction, the more that returns to us.

Specifically, it is my understanding that there are three main ways in which we benefit from prayer. I will put them in what I perceive to be their order of importance:

---

21. *Avos* 3:8

1. We get to stand in Hashem's presence and have a relationship with Him directly.
2. It is a process of self-clarification.
3. When we do receive something, we are in a position to appreciate that it comes from Hashem.

There is a fourth aspect, which is only a side benefit, but a benefit nevertheless, and that is that our prayers, when answered, provide us with that which we ask for. I will talk about this later.

Relationship with Hashem

To pray is to communicate with the Infinite. Take a moment to think of what that means. We little ants can talk to Hashem Almighty, the Creator of time, space, and matter; the Transcendent Being; the Infinite, Formless Truth of the universe. The concept alone should blow our minds, let alone the application. When a human being stands in prayer, there is no one else in the world other than him and Hashem. He has Hashem's full and complete attention. It is his own private audience with the King of kings. And that audience is available wherever and whenever we request — at a moment's notice!

As I've said already, at its core, prayer is a spiritual experience. It is a time to experience Hashem's presence in a tangible and genuine way. It's a time for the spiritual essence of a human being to soar into the heavens and bask in Hashem's holiness.[22] Above and beyond all else, this is the ultimate meaning of prayer — its most precious gift.[23]

SELF-CLARIFICATION

The word for prayer in Hebrew is להתפלל. It is a reflexive verb, the root of which is פלל, which means "judge."[24] Being that the Hebrew word for prayer is a reflexive verb, it therefore means "to judge oneself." It is a process of

---

22. In a final response to the question of whether we should be praying in the format of "Let me not be presumptuous, Hashem, to ask for what I want, rather, I will simply ask you to give me what I need," I would like to add the following point. Prayer is about connecting to Hashem. A person who does not have children and desperately wants them, such as Chanah, will pour out his heart in desperation before Hashem. A person whose loved one is sick will do the same. This is the expression of the relationship, that is prayer's purpose. But let me ask, could a person pour his heart out and cry genuine tears, as they might if praying for a child who is dying, while saying the prayer above? If a person could, and only if they could, then such a person would indeed be someone for whom this is, as the *Sefer HaIkrim* says, "the most fitting form of prayer." But I think that is a massively high level, and personally, I would recommend sticking with specific prayers as a means of connecting to Hashem, rather than generic ones.

23. I once asked my rebbe why is it that even though (as I explain later) the format of prayer is that of praise, request, and thanks, nevertheless we are told (*Orach Chaim* 101:1) that one fulfills his obligation of prayer if he has *kavanah* only in the first blessing of *Shemoneh Esrei* (which contains only praise). He answered me that the format of prayer is indeed the aforementioned three elements, however, the essence and ultimate purpose of prayer is that one connect to Hashem. Saying only the first blessing of *Shemoneh Esrei* with *kavanah* would certainly accomplish this. Rav Shimshon Pincus touches on something similar in *She'arim B'Tefillah* (pp. 48–49), saying that ultimately, prayer is about *hisbatlus*, recognizing Hashem as the ultimate power in the universe. Asking Hashem for all of our needs is, of course, an expression of this — perhaps the simplest and most obvious expression, as it is inherent in the act rather than something one is trying to experience. Accordingly, asking is simply a recognition of Hashem's greatness. The first blessing of *Shemoneh Esrei* accomplishes this directly. While *only* having *kavanah* in the first blessing is by no means recommended, it cannot be said that it does not achieve the purpose of prayer if one had prayed in such a way.

24. As we see in the verse וְנָתַן בִּפְלִלִים, "according to the judges" (*Shemos* 21:22).

self-clarification. Prayer's focus is clarifying and intensifying our commitment to what it is that we really want.

How exactly one does this, I will explain later.

Appreciating That It Comes from Hashem

This one is pretty simple. If you don't ask for anything from Hashem, then when you receive something, you might think it came to you via other means. Conversely, if we ask Hashem for what we need, when we receive what we requested, it helps us appreciate where it came from. It's by no means foolproof, but it certainly helps. Prayer can help us to find the humility required for genuine gratitude.

An Answer to Our Requests

The fourth aspect, as I mentioned above, is a side benefit and nothing more. It is the actual change in reality we can initiate through prayer. When Moshe prayed to Hashem after the incident of the Golden Calf, he was able to save the entire Jewish nation. Hashem's will was to destroy them, and Moshe — through the power of prayer alone — saved them.

When Choni HaMe'agel prayed, he had no doubt that rain would come.[25] In fact, he specified the exact amount of rain. For a man as proficient in prayer as Choni, prayer is like a tap. The amount of blessing that comes out is directly dependent on how much you turn it.

---

25. *Taanis* 19b

— CHAPTER 1 —

For the vast majority of us, though, there isn't quite the same guarantee — some you win and some you lose — but for those who know what they are doing, like Moshe and Choni HaMe'agel, it is pure science.

Jump off a building and you fall. Pray and it rains. There is no difference.

The Medrash tells us that "anyone who prays a great deal will be answered."[26] It's not "may be answered" but "will be answered." It's unequivocal. This Medrash does not refer only to Choni and those like him. It says "anyone." We just need to "pray" and mean it in our heart — and do it over and over again until we're answered.[27]

However, all of this, as I said above, is merely a side benefit. It would be circular reasoning to believe that Hashem made us lacking in life in order that we can pray and then have our needs provided for. There must be some purpose to the process of prayer beyond getting our needs fulfilled, otherwise Hashem would not have made the lack in the first place.

For example, if Hashem wanted Chanah to have a child and there was nothing more that He wanted from Chanah, then why would He make her barren simply in order that she should pray and then receive the child that Hashem wanted her to have in the first place? Why not just give her the child? Obviously, when Hashem creates a lack, it is so that we will pray to Him, but the things for which we are praying are only means to a greater purpose.

Hashem could just as well have provided for all of our needs and wants in the first place and skipped our need

---

26. *Yalkut Shimoni, Shmuel I* 1:1

27. I believe there are exceptions to this rule, though limited. It is beyond the scope of this book to go into the mechanics of how they might work. Suffice to say that in almost all circumstances, if you pray, Hashem will answer.

to prayer, unless, of course, there is a purpose to prayer beyond simply having it answered. Indeed, He gave us prayer for the three reasons above. And He makes us lack in certain areas so that we can pray and grow in the ways described. But, ultimately, the three reasons above point to a single factor: for us to develop our relationship with Hashem. This is the ultimate goal of prayer.

If we grow and benefit in the way that we need to through prayer, then there is usually no reason that our prayers should not be answered — as the purpose of the lack in the first place has been achieved. But, as Hashem considers many factors far beyond what we can possibly perceive, there is never any guarantee.

Self-Clarification

I'd like to go more deeply now into the second aspect of prayer that I talked about above: self-clarification, or judgment. It is the one with the most practical ramifications on the actual process of praying.

More than that, it is the means through which we achieve the first goal also: a relationship with Hashem. In other words, prayer is not simply experiencing Hashem. That is part of the mitzvah of *emunah* (faith), as the verse says, "*Shivisi Hashem lenegdi samid* — I visualize Hashem before me always."[28] Prayer is something different. Although its goal is to experience Hashem, the application comes through the medium of our conversations with Hashem.

Understanding what this concept means will start to point us in the direction of how we can pray and come to

---

28. *Tehillim* 16:8

mean it. Here's where we start to move from the theory and philosophy into the practical application.

As a basis for my discussion of this topic, I want to use three points that my rebbe, Rabbi Noach Weinberg z"l, used to remind me as absolutely fundamental in prayer. We will talk about each one as we go along.

1. Be Specific

As I have mentioned above, we should be specific about what we want. At the basic level of prayer that most of us are functioning on, it is too easy to simply ask Hashem to do His will as He sees fit without any personal elucidation. We need to want things, and then talk to Hashem about those things that we want.

2. Why?

We must explain why we want what we want. If we don't have good enough reasons to justify it for ourselves, why would we go before Hashem and ask for something that we have not put thought into or considered whether we really want it?

3. Be a Partner

We cannot simply ask Hashem for something, then lie in bed and wait for it to happen.[29] We must take responsibility and do our very best to do the job

---

29. Granted, the Medrash tells us (*Eichah Rabbah* 1:30) that this is precisely what Chizkiyahu did when he went to sleep with the Assyrian army surrounding Yerushalayim and left it entirely up to Hashem, but the Medrash is using him as an example of a lofty level of trust in Hashem. When we are at that level, it is something that we can perhaps consider. Until such a time, I'm afraid we will need to drag ourselves out of bed.

ourselves, while praying and trusting that Hashem is the One Who ultimately controls our world. At the same time, we must know that if things do go our way, that is *only* because Hashem allowed it to happen (perhaps as a result of our prayer), and not through our own strengths or skills alone.

I will not address each of these as a topic, rather, I will include the ideas throughout the following pages.

So, what is meant by self-clarification?

Theoretical ideas are always less clear than ideas that we have to articulate. It often happens to me that I'm sure something is clear to me, but the minute I start to try to explain it to someone else, I realize that I don't properly understand it yet. So too with what we want. Articulating to Hashem why something matters to us forces us to be clearer in our own minds as to why it matters to us and, by so doing, helps us become more sincere and more determined. (Or, conversely, we might realize that it doesn't matter as much as we thought it did.)

Let me use an example.

Josh wants to pass an exam tomorrow. So, he stands before Hashem and prays that he will have the understanding to answer the questions correctly.

But that is obviously not enough if he wants his prayer to be meaningful. Hashem is not a vending machine where we put our prayer into the slot and our request is fulfilled at the bottom.[30] We have to show Him that we are serious.

---

30. Even though this might sound like what happened above with Choni HaMe'agel, Choni did not simply say the words of prayer and achieve the result. As the story tells us, this was only a part of a deep and sophisticated relationship that Choni had with Hashem.

After all, if it doesn't mean enough to us, why would it mean anything to Him?[31]

So, back to our example. Josh has to explain why he wants to pass the exam. He wants to pass the exam because it means a great deal to him.

But what *exactly* does it mean to him? The process of Josh's conversation with Hashem might go something along these lines:

Well, I need it in order to get into university.

Talk more about that . . .

I want to go to university in order to be able to make a living.

Carry on . . .

I want to live a meaningful life and know it will be difficult without a stable income, and that is dependent on university, which is dependent on passing this exam.

OK, now we're talking. Prayer is starting to force Josh to understand himself.

If he thinks a bit further, he might conclude that he also does not want to be seen as a failure. It hurts to be seen as a failure, and he doesn't want to go through that pain.

And he wants to make his parents proud.

And he wants to feel good about himself.

We could understand if a father decides to say no to a son who simply wants to pass an exam without understanding why; doing so might make him arrogant or lazy or overconfident. But to a son who wants to live a meaningful life,

---

31. This is clear in the example with Choni HaMe'agel. He drew a circle around himself and said he would not move until Hashem answered the Jewish people. A man such as Choni HaMe'agel does not make empty promises. He would have been willing to die in that circle had Hashem not sent rain. Similarly, Moshe, in his prayers after the Golden Calf and after the episode with the Spies, did not simply ask for the Jewish people to be spared; he explained to Hashem why He simply had no choice but to spare them.

who doesn't want the pain of failure, who wants to make his parents proud . . . it is much harder for a father to say no to that![32]

The more a person verbalizes his reasons, the more he feels the need to have that which he is praying for. And the more he feels the need, the more Hashem feels his need, so to speak. And the more Hashem feels his need, the more likely He is to respond positively.

If something would just be nice for us, Hashem may give it to us anyway. But if it becomes a desperate need, it is much more likely to elicit a positive response. Simply stated, the more it means to us, the more it means to Hashem, so to speak.

The bottom line of prayer is that we need to show Hashem that we are serious. If we are just playing games — immaturely asking for anything that we see and want as if we're children in a candy store — He will not necessarily respond. (I say "necessarily" because at the end of the day, Hashem loves each of us deeply, and parents sometimes give gifts to their children for no reason other than that they love them. And at the same time, sometimes they deny their kids things because they know better what is healthy and not healthy for them.) But if we are serious people trying to live serious lives, this is what Hashem is looking for. And, of course, He will be a lot more likely to respond.

This is the concept of self-clarification. It gives us clarity on who we are and what matters to us and makes us deeper and more serious people.

---

32. I believe that as the process of prayer pushes what we want more and more in line with the meaningful life that Hashem wants for us, it becomes "harder" and "harder" for Him to say no. Is there a magical point at which it becomes a certainty for Hashem to say yes? That's an interesting philosophical question. Either way, however, continued sincere prayer has the power to make the result that we are looking for more and more likely.

— CHAPTER 1 —

And, by the way, serious prayer can, and sometimes will, take a person in a different direction.

Let's return to Josh on the night before his big exam. Another way the conversation with Hashem might look can have surprising results.

Let's say that he is praying to pass his exam and starts considering why he is taking it. To go to university. But why? The answer comes back that everyone goes to university and he does not want to be different.

So, Hashem, please don't make me be different is the beginning of his prayer.

But that doesn't sound good enough, so he considers further. Maybe sometimes it's good to be different. Maybe he needs to know what he really wants from life, rather than just following the crowd . . .

OK, Hashem, there is no harm in my failing the exam, but I'd like to take the time to pray to You for something that really matters to me. Please help me to know what I am living for and what matters to me.

There is another important element in showing Hashem that we are serious and we mean it, and that is to figure out, during prayer, what more we could be doing ourselves and not just leaving things up to Hashem. For example, let's take a man who is struggling in his marriage and he is praying to Hashem for assistance. His prayer might go as follows.

Hashem, I want my marriage to be more successful than it is. I want it because I can't stand the thought of divorce, because it will be hell for the kids, because my wife really does mean so much to me, because I care for her and I want it to work . . .

This all sounds good and genuine. But then he might honestly ask himself:

But what am I doing? How hard am I trying? What do I want from me?

With such introspection, he may come to the following conclusion:

Well, I suppose I could and probably should leave work early for the next week and spend the extra time sitting and talking with her. And what about if I called my wife a few times a day from the office instead of waiting for her to get in touch with me and then getting annoyed that she called me at work? That would probably be a good idea and show some genuine intent to save this relationship.

And if he continues in his thoughts, he might come to further ideas to help his marriage:

And how about if I write a list of my wife's virtues and go over it three times a day? I know these things might help, and I know I should do them . . .

Surely a person cannot seriously go before Hashem and ask for help if he is not even trying to help himself! Part of prayer — and it's a big part of prayer — is "discussing" with Hashem how we are going to help ourselves.

Just imagine you go in front of a king to beg for his assistance. You are a loyal subject, and he is willing to give you a hearing. Your family is starving and you ask if please, please, he could help you.

"Why is your family starving?" he asks. "Why do you have no money?"

Well, you have had a few jobs, but have been too lazy to stick to them. You got an inheritance but gambled it away. And you have a large check that someone gave you waiting to be cashed, but you just can't find the time to go to the bank. So you'd really appreciate some cash.

Not only would the king not help you, he would have you thrown out and told never to return.

Now, Hashem is our Father as well as our King, so we have a bit more leeway in terms of His mercy. However, it is still ridiculous to beg Him for help if we are not at least trying to help ourselves.

We need to show Hashem that we are serious, and part of that process is seeing if there is anything more that we could be doing to help us achieve what we need.

This is a constant process. When we pray in this way, the prayer never stagnates, it develops. We come back the next day with a more developed conversation.

Look, Hashem, I called my wife three times. I left work early. OK, I didn't write the list yet. But I'm really trying. I'm really serious . . .

A week later:

Hashem, I'm really going at it. But where are You? Things aren't getting any better . . .

Maybe there is more I can do? OK, Hashem, here's my next level of commitment. I know I can do more, but please, please, please help me to do so . . . I know I'm failing. I know I only came home early once last week and I still didn't write my list, but please, Hashem, I'm trying so hard.

Which father could refuse such a child? A child who says he is desperate and he is trying, but he just doesn't feel that he can do it on his own . . .

This is the power of prayer.

It stems from the premise that we have a Father in Heaven Who wants to give us everything. But, like a good father, He wants what is best for His child, and what is best is that his child knows why he wants what he wants.

Let's say my seventeen-year-old son comes to me and says he wants a Ferrari. And let's say I can afford it (now, there's something to pray for!). Why does he want a Ferrari? I ask. He wants to drive fast on the highway, show off to his friends, and be the most popular guy in town. Well, he didn't do a great job of convincing me on that one. I know that if I give it to him, he will likely end up crashing it and hurting himself and maybe others also.

"Go back and think about that one again," I tell him.

The next week he is back again. He thought about it and realized I am right. If he's going to get a Ferrari, he needs to value and appreciate it. So, here's his next try. He loves the look and feel of the car. He's struggling to find friends right now, and the car would help. He has driven many cars, but has enjoyed none as much as the Ferrari. And he will take care of it and drive it responsibly, as there is no one who would want to crash it less than he.

OK, he's moving in the right direction. That sounds at least palatable to me. But the answer is still no. Back to the drawing board.

The next week he is back again.

He has just started a *chessed* project. He needs to get very quickly from place to place in order that he can help even more people in the limited hours he has available. He really wants to use the car to make a difference for others who need his help.

Now, that's a bit farfetched, but assuming that I check out his story and it matches up, he's certainly upped his chances.

Hashem is "*bochen klayos valev* — searches within [our] kidneys and [our] hearts." He checks out our stories to see if they match what is in our hearts. We can pay lip service to people, but Hashem knows, without a doubt, whether we mean it or not. So, for my son, Hashem would be checking if he is genuine about the *chessed* project, or if it's just another excuse to get me to buy him the car. With Hashem, there is no way around sincerity. The more that

Chapter 1

our words and our hearts are one, the more likely He will take us seriously. The goal here is not to convince ourselves that we are right, but to have an honest conversation with ourselves about our true needs and desires.

Hashem loves us. He wants us to have everything, and He has everything to give — money, success, wonderful relationships, health, our children's future . . . It's all constantly in stock on His distribution shelves.

There is only one prerequisite: we have to be serious and want it all for genuine reasons. We have to be people who will appreciate it when we receive it, and not become complacent. We have to show Him — no, not really to show Him, but show ourselves — that what we want matters. We have to know why it matters. And it has to matter enough for us to be ready to struggle to make it happen ourselves. At that point, we are in with an excellent chance of Hashem saying yes.

In fact, a man such as Choni HaMe'agel, who has perfected all of this within himself, can tell people to bring in their Pesach ovens before he prays, because he knows, quite simply, that when he starts praying, it *is* going to rain.

Chapter 2
Connecting to the Power of Prayer

    We have a friend who is very sick and we want him to get better, so we pray for him.

    We might start our prayer with the fact that he has children who need him and are suffering. And his wife is a good woman who cares deeply for her husband and needs him desperately. As we explain more and more, the feeling of connection to the person and the situation deepens, and this in turn deepens the feeling of need in our heart and mind. As we continue to mention all of the good that this person has done in his life, as well as the people he has helped and the good that we are sure he will do in the future if he will be healthy, our prayer becomes more and more meaningful and powerful as our feeling becomes stronger.

    Once we have explained properly to Hashem why we think he should get better, the next question should be, what are we going to do ourselves to aid his recovery? We are going to visit him to try to cheer him up. We are going to get a group together to pray for him. We are going to make sure he is getting the best treatment . . . We don't have to do all of these things specifically. Not everything will always be appropriate. But the more we do, the more we show Hashem that we mean it when we say that we want him to get better. By conducting our prayer in this manner, we are not just paying lip service to the idea of praying for our friend.

In addition, there is value to mentioning the name — especially the Hebrew name — of the person in our prayer. It is a strong and established custom to do so, and it shows that we care about who he is. Also, the Rabbis tell us that using the sick person's name together with his mother's name in prayer evokes mercy in and of itself. But that is still only the *form* of the prayer — the words that we couch the prayer in; what is much more important is the *quality* of the prayer, and that quality is created by meaning what we say. If we really do care, then firstly, we will know and be able to articulate why it matters to us, and secondly, we will be ready to do what we can to help.

This does not mean we always have to try to help. If we became involved actively with everything and everyone we prayed for, we wouldn't have time for anything else. However, we need to make a choice where this prayer lies in our priorities. And based on that, we should then put sufficient time and energy into getting our prayer answered.

As a result, it should go without saying that if someone gives us the name of someone to pray for, the more we can know about the person, the more we will mean what we pray for them. If someone merely tells us that Moshe ben Sarah is sick, it's a name on a piece of paper. Yes, if we have a deep love for humanity, we will recognize that it is a person, a soul, and that may well suffice. But for the vast majority of us (myself at least) who do not yet feel that deep sense of connection to a theoretical soul, we need more information in order to feel the connection.

So, let's say we're told that Moshe ben Sarah has seven young children, he has always been a good man and a pillar of his community, he has a young wife who is in a great deal of pain, and his illness is very serious. A more three-dimensional person like this is someone to whom we can certainly feel more attached and for whom we can pray much more meaningfully.

So, what happens, as is often the case, if you are only given a name and asked to pray for this person's recovery? There is a very simple solution: ask for more information! If I am asked to pray for someone and I want to respond, I will always make it my business to find out more — not to be nosey, but because I personally find it very hard to pray for a name, no matter how lovely a name it might be! Our prayer will take on a whole new dimension once we can picture and connect to the one whom we are praying for.

Aren't Some Things Too Unimportant to Pray for?

This question is very common. At its root is a fundamental misunderstanding of Hashem and our relationship with Him.

To suggest that something is unimportant to pray for is to suggest that some things don't matter to Hashem. From a Jewish perspective, this borders on, and probably even crosses the line of, heresy.

To think that Hashem does not care about something means that we believe that He is not involved in it — and

— CHAPTER 2 —

if He is not involved in it, there is some sense of it happening without Hashem. That idea is antithetical to Jewish philosophy.

Nothing in this world happens without Hashem's active input. Hence, if it is a part of the world, that means Hashem is aware of it and consciously making it happen. The fact that something exists means that Hashem wants it to exist.

Essentially, the question of something being too unimportant to pray for would, therefore, be answered according to whether something was too unimportant for Hashem to deal with. I don't believe there is a concept of "big" or "small" for Hashem. If it's in Hashem's world, it's important — whether it's Yankel's toothache, a game of football, or peace between nations. Nothing is too difficult for Hashem to do, nothing takes up more of His time, and nothing is too small for Him to be concerned about. Human beings need to have priorities because we cannot do everything. Hashem, Who is unlimited by time and space, needs no priorities, as everything that He wills, He is able to do, immediately. Hashem is never "busy" doing something else.

Hence, nothing is too small or insignificant for Hashem to be interested in. And, most certainly, nothing is so insignificant that it is overlooked by Hashem. If Hashem is not conscious of something, then it simply does not exist. Everything that exists, from the smallest microbe thousands of meters under the sea in Antarctica to the farthest star that is just a speck in the night sky, is relevant to Hashem.

The verse in *Tehillim* says that Hashem is close to those who "call to Him in truth."[33] It does not mention what they are calling to Him about. What matters is that it matters to them — and Hashem responds. How relevant it should be to

---

33. *Tehillim* 145:18

us is another matter entirely, and this is what prayer comes to address. And it is another example of where prayer clarifies and develops our priorities and values.

Let's take an inane example:

Should I pray for my soccer team to win?

So, let's start with the facts again. Does Hashem care who wins? Yes, He very much does — but likely for very different reasons than I would care who wins. He doesn't randomly support a team because He was born in the team's city. He sees a macro picture and where a soccer match fits into that picture and how who wins will have an effect on a global level.

Hashem cares who wins — but should I care who wins? That's a completely different question and one that prayer will be very helpful in answering.

So, it's important to me, for one reason or another, that my team win. Now, I could simply say to myself, "That's ridiculous; let's move on to something more relevant than twenty-two men trying to kick a sphere of inflated leather between two posts." However, this does not deal with the fact that somewhere inside of me it genuinely matters (otherwise I would not care if my team wins or not). Through prayer, I might actually come to the conclusion that caring who wins is a waste of time — but it would then be something that I genuinely feel, not something I am paying lip service to because I believe it in theory.

So let's see how prayer might be helpful.

I sit down, close my eyes and start to pray intently.

Dear Hashem, Almighty Father, King of this entire universe, I beg You, I beseech you, I humbly turn my heart to you — please, please, please let my team win today.

As I say it, it might sound a little off already, but let's move on to the next step, which is explaining why.

Why do I want this, Hashem?

Personally, I get a little stuck at that point, but let's keep going for the sake of illustration.

Because my team matters to me!

Why is that?

Because they always have.

And . . . ?

Because I feel happy when they win, and I want to feel happy today.

And my team winning will mean a lot to many other people also.

(Likely I'm forgetting here that if my team does indeed win, there will be a similar number of people whose team lost and are feeling miserable as a result — but let's put that part aside for the moment and carry on.)

So, Hashem, I've got it clear now: it will make me happy and many others happy also. Surely that's a good reason to make it happen?

But as I delve deeper into my true needs, I start to think . . .

But is that real happiness? Is it a lasting feeling of good, or is it just a high until the next game?

Hmmm . . . that's an uncomfortable question.

I suppose it's not the best way to gain happiness. True happiness is connection to You, and my team winning doesn't really contribute to that . . .

(There might be more stages to go through, but I'm going to cut through to a likely ending, whatever the middle might look like.)

OK, I guess maybe my team winning is not as important to me as I thought it was. Come to think of it, it would be nice if they win, but I guess it's not so terrible if they lose, and if it's true happiness that I'm looking for, it might be a better idea to look elsewhere . . .

Prayer has the potential to clarify what matters to me and what doesn't.

So, yes, prayer is a request for anything and everything that we might want. But it is more than that, because as we sincerely stand before Hashem, clarity and perspective start to develop, and what we want often starts to change.

This back-and-forth is actually the first form of prayer that we are going to talk about. It is what the Rabbis call *sichah* — conversation.

But in simple terms, what matters to me matters to Hashem, and the more I show Hashem that it matters to me, the more likely He will respond. The verse in *Tehillim* says that Hashem is close to those who "call to Him in truth." It does not mention what they are calling to Him about. What matters is that it matters to them — and Hashem responds.

A good friend of mine told me of an elderly woman who was his neighbor in Poland. She had lost her husband years ago and had no children and very few friends. All she had for company was a bird which she cared for lovingly. One day, her bird died. She sat down and began to pray. She cried until her eyes were dry of tears. My friend, among many others, told her there was no point in praying because the bird was dead. Perhaps they could buy her a new one, but this one was not coming back. Well, they were wrong, because the next day the bird was alive and kicking again.

As fantastical as this story may sound, and as uncommon such a phenomenon is, part of prayer is believing that although He may choose not to, Hashem *can* make it happen. Hashem listens to those who call to Him in truth.

It does not matter what it is about. What matters is the relationship. And if there is a relationship, then Hashem responds.

Of course, we human beings would want to consider the value of a bird compared to other things that might matter more. To this woman, the bird meant a lot, but for others, it may be a shame to spend their lives worrying about birds and not, say, world peace! But we are human, and what matters to us matters to us. If prayer shifts our focus to something more meaningful, then all the better. But if it does not — then we should call out to Hashem for what matters to us, no matter what it might be. Because the calling out itself is the way we connect to Hashem.

Please, Hashem, Help Me to Steal

There is one area where I would say that prayer is inappropriate, and that is asking Hashem to help us do something that we know to be morally wrong.

For example: *Please, Hashem, help me to steal.*

As Hashem is infinite, it is He who enables a person to steal when he chooses to do so. As the Gemara tells us, "Hashem leads a person in the way he desires to go." Asking for His assistance, therefore, is acknowledging that we can do nothing without His input — even steal. Hence, there is value in doing so. Better a thief who recognizes that Hashem runs the world than a thief who believes that he himself runs the world.

However, stealing is a choice that one makes. The stealer shows Hashem that he "desires" it, and then He carries out the action for him in response — hence "leading" him in the way he "desires" to go.

How do we show Hashem that we desire something? One way is by taking action to try to make it happen. A second is by praying. Just as one should not take action to steal — thus showing Hashem he is serious about it — so should he not pray to be able to steal, thus also indicating to Hashem that he means it. Doing an evil act is the same activation of desire as praying for it (assuming that one prays and means it, rather than simply paying lip service).

This does not mean that praying will not help one to be a successful thief. Hashem listens to our prayers — for better and for worse — and responds. But a prayer for evil is an act of evil — and wrong in and of itself.

Praying for Bad and the Evil Eye

Bilaam, an evil prophet who lived at the time of the Exodus from Egypt, was hired by Balak, king of Mo'av, to curse the Jewish people when they were wandering in the desert. Bilaam asked Hashem if he could go, and Hashem forbade him. However, through his insistent praying, Hashem eventually allowed him to go. Ultimately, Hashem did not allow him to curse the Jewish people, as the Jewish people were not worthy of a curse. But his prayer enabled him to go through the motions of doing an evil act that Hashem would otherwise not have allowed him to do.

Bilaam's prayer is an example of one aspect of what Judaism refers to as the evil eye.

Chapter 2

The Gemara gives the example of walking by someone's field at harvest time.[34] A person might become resentful and wish, so to speak, that the crops do not succeed. He might be horrified that he feels this, but he does. And he feels it sincerely. And, as we have said earlier, Hashem responds to sincerity, for better and for worse.

This is a subconscious prayer, but Hashem listens to the subconscious just as much as He listens to the conscious. The person is willing, begging almost, for the crops to fail. And such a "prayer" can have an effect.

Another example might be when one boasts about his children in front of a childless couple. One or both of them might subconsciously feel that the parent doesn't deserve to have children if he is that insensitive. Again, horrified as they might be if they realized that they thought such a thing, they might nevertheless; because of the pain of their own childlessness, they mean it genuinely and sincerely in their hearts. It might become, almost by accident, a situation of "Hashem is close to all those who cry to Him, to all those who cry to Him in truth." The "truth" of this person's pain compels Hashem to listen to his inner complaint against the one causing that pain, and He responds accordingly.

In prayer, we human beings have been handed a very powerful means through which to change the reality of both ourselves and our world. As with anything else in the world, the more power it has for positive, the more power it has for negative.

---

34. *Bava Metzia* 107a

Praying for Others and Free Will

We Jews believe that so-called "bad things" happen to people for a reason. (This issue is the subject of my previous book, *Why Bad Things Don't Happen to Good People*.) If a person, for example, gets sick, that is because Hashem wants him to be sick. It is for his benefit in some way — either it is a message for him, a means of humbling him, an atonement, or a test — there are lots of possibilities. But one way or another, it is there to benefit him.

If so, who am I to pray for him to get better? What might look like a good idea to me (for this person to be healthy) is clearly not a good idea in the eyes of Hashem — because if Hashem wanted him to be healthy, then he *would* be healthy.

The idea of a person praying for himself is more readily understandable. As he changes his perspective and priorities through his prayer, he grows as a person and changes himself enough to become a person who no longer needs to be ill. But how does that work with someone else praying for him?

Firstly, we human beings are all connected, and all one entity. And the Jewish people, all the more so, are different parts of a single soul. As such, we have the ability to affect each other.

Furthermore, when I pray for someone else, I do much the same as I do for myself, despite the fact that I obviously can't change how that person sees the world.

I try to find reasons why Hashem should help him. The person is a loving father and his children need him, for instance. He is kindhearted and contributes so much — the

Chapter 2

world needs him. He supports his family — what would they do without him?

But more than this, I believe it is important to talk about what I am going to do to improve this person's situation. *I will be a partner with You, Hashem. If this man needs to learn a lesson, let me be the one to teach him rather than his illness. I will reach out to him and try to see how I might be able to help him grow. I will spend time with him and assist him.* Ultimately, there may be nothing I can do to help. But proper prayer will lead me to that conclusion, rather than just assuming that I can't play a role in his recovery from the beginning. And, I have usually found that with people I genuinely care to pray for, there *is* something that we can do.[35]

You might say that you don't have time for all of this, and that may well be true. But if we care and genuinely want to reach out to and help other people, it requires more than simply mentioning a one-dimensional Hebrew name in a prayer list.[36] The effect that we have in this world is commensurate with the choices we make and the effort we invest. Little investment means little return. A mentioned name in a busy prayer service will, most likely, have comparatively minimal effect. Standing before Hashem and begging Him on behalf of others, in the way that Avraham

---

35. It goes without saying that even when there is nothing we can do, we can, and should, still pray. I'm saying that prayer without effort to do something to help is somewhat disingenuous. But if there is really nothing we can do, then prayer can be completely genuine even though we are doing nothing to help.

36. Of course, there is a concept of a short prayer making a difference, such as Moshe's prayer for his sister Miriam, which was all of five words. But that is for someone with great proficiency in prayer. A master of prayer might mention a name and genuinely mean the prayer for that soul without even knowing the person. Hence, that prayer would have a significant effect. But for most of us, that's just not realistic, and simply mentioning a name without any context to the prayer will be of limited value.

did on behalf of Sodom, is likely to really make a difference. And I am quite confident that had Hashem actually saved Sodom, Avraham would have put in more effort to reach out to them once he realized that Hashem had been ready to destroy them.

I don't know of any actual obligation to pray on behalf of another individual other than the mitzvah to do *chessed*. But if you are moved to do so, then do so with effort and engagement, not simply half-hearted ritual.

Personally, if someone asks me to pray for someone whom I do not know, the name is not what I will ask for first (although, as I said above, praying for a name is customary). What I'm much more interested in is knowing something about the person, information that will give me something specific to pray about and will help me mean what I say. I might ask the person's age, his illness, or his prognosis. Does he have children, and if yes, what are their ages? I find that the more information that I can glean, the more I can stand before Hashem and implore Him genuinely on the person's behalf. I am not at the level whereby a name means something to me as it might to greater men, but human suffering does mean something to me, and this type of information is what I need to know if I am to pray in a way that might be of significant benefit to the person I am praying for.

The Atheist's Prayer

As I mentioned above, the verse says that "Hashem is close to all those who call to Him — to all who call to him *in truth*." The words "in truth" are the essence of what prayer is about. Prayer is about calling to Hashem, and sincerity is what Hashem responds to.

I heard the following story numerous times from Rabbi Noach Weinberg. Rabbi Weinberg referred to the story as "The Atheist's Prayer."

In the 1970s, a young American Jew called Jeff came to visit Eretz Yisrael. He was studying for his MBA at Harvard University. Although he was a devout atheist, he nevertheless came to the Western Wall to see an ancient historical monument. While he had seen a few monuments that were equally old, if not older, this one affected him deeply. He felt touched by the experience. But it did not make sense to him, as an atheist, that some old stones could have this effect on him. It occurred to him to say this prayer:

God, I don't believe that You exist. However, I am feeling something here that I never thought I would, so just in case You do exist, please give me some sort of sign to show me.

No sooner had the words come out of his mouth than a hand tapped him on the shoulder.

"Would you like to visit a yeshivah?" the owner of the hand said to him when he turned around.

"What is a yeshivah?" responded Jeff.

"A place where you learn about God."

Given what he had just prayed and this immediate response, Jeff felt he had no choice, so he came up the steps to Aish HaTorah Yeshivah. He met Rabbi Weinberg and was so impressed that he ended up studying there for six weeks. He discovered not only Hashem, but a passion for Judaism to boot.

Not long before he left Eretz Yisrael to head back to Boston, he noticed a lovely, young religious girl at the Western Wall. He felt there was something special about her, something pure and real. He prayed again — though not as an atheist this time — and asked Hashem that he be allowed to find a girl like this.

He returned to Boston and a few weeks later was in the local synagogue and glanced over the partition into the ladies' section. Unbelievably, that same young girl was standing right there, in Boston. He introduced himself after the service, and one thing led to another. They married and built a religious home together.

Why did Hashem listen to Jeff's prayers and respond so obviously and immediately? Because Jeff was sincere. It was not just lip service. When someone tapped him on the shoulder and told him that he could come and learn about Hashem, he accepted the invitation immediately. When he saw the girl again, he went up to her right away. Even as an atheist, he was ready to call out to Hashem in truth, and Hashem answered him.

Kavanah

Kavanah — intention — is the essence of prayer. As the *Chovos HaLevavos* says, "Prayer without intent is like a body without a soul."[37]

However, one cannot simply command focus and intention. We live in a world with many distractions. How does one concentrate and feel connected when he prays?

I want to tell you a story that happened to me a little while ago. Something similar happens regularly, but this was a very remarkable example so I mention it here.

I returned from work one day in a pretty low mood. Nothing in particular happened, I just felt down. In this state of mind, my world was not looking great and so,

---

37. *Chovos HaLevavos* 8:3

Chapter 2

somewhat inevitably, I had an argument with my wife and then went to bed early.

I awoke the next day and wanted to curl up in bed and not face the world. Then my teenage son knocked on my door to ask me to come to shul with him. Wasn't it supposed to be the opposite with fathers and teenage sons? He should be curling up in a bed and I should be knocking on his door. That thought got me up, and I went to shul with him.

On the way, I realized that in the state of mind I was in, I was going to pray with no meaning whatsoever. I would simply be going through the motions. On the one hand, the halachah nowadays tells me to pray even if I will have no *kavanah*. Nevertheless, this is certainly not ideal, and there is part of me that deeply dislikes praying without meaning.

So as we made our way to shul, I tried to get myself into a better state of mind. Well, good luck with that one, Shaul. How many times in my life had I been in a bad mood and actually talked myself out of it? If I'm honest, the answer is never. But that didn't stop me from trying.

So, I had a conversation with myself — or rather, I gave myself a lecture:

I can't feel like this; I mustn't feel like this. It's a big mitzvah to be happy.

Still miserable.

Come on, Hashem loves me. I should be feeling great.

Now I was feeling worse because I *should* be feeling so grateful, but I wasn't.

I got to shul and started going through the motions but found my mood dropping further and further. Here I was, speaking to Hashem, or rather, saying words to Hashem — and feeling nothing. It seemed like the further I got into the davening, the worse I felt. Nothing was helping.

Still miserable. The more I tried to force myself into a better feeling, the worse I felt.

But I was there and I was saying the words at least, going through the motions. For some strange reason, I kept trying to push myself to feel differently. How often has that worked for me in my life? By my rough estimate zero. But the statistics didn't stop me from trying.

The end of *Pesukei D'Zimra* — miserable.

Barchu — miserable.

Shema — miserable.

Now I was getting a little desperate.

Am I going to go through this entire davening feeling miserable and disconnected? C'mon, Shemoneh Esrei *is coming up; it's now or never.*

End of *Shema* — miserable.

Tzur Yisrael — surely it was now or never?

As I came toward the *brachah* of *Gaal Yisrael*, I realized it wasn't going to happen for me. But as I realized that, I suddenly had another realization.

I've been battling since I woke up so that I can feel kavanah in my davening. But maybe I don't need to? Maybe Hashem doesn't want me to? Maybe, instead of fighting Hashem, I would be better off going along with His plan?

This was not something I had to convince myself of. It was something I saw clearly for myself — and that was different from everything I had been doing that morning so far. Until that point, it had been about me. *I* want to daven with *kavanah*; *I* wanted to feel better; *I* wanted to connect to Hashem. *I, I, I, I*. Subtly but surely, the ego had been driving me — in the guise of holiness. Suddenly, I had realized that *I* didn't matter. I could daven without *kavanah* if that was what Hashem wanted from me. I could serve Him in that way also.

— CHAPTER 2 —

I let go. I was fully willing to say meaningless words and feel nothing, even feel miserable if that was what was expected of me . . .

And in that moment, my ego was gone and my soul returned. I felt lifted out of my body, and I have rarely been more connected than that day as I started *Shemoneh Esrei*. It was a beautiful *Shemoneh Esrei*, and I was still davening it after everyone else had gone home from shul.

Now let me tell you another story and I will come to my point.

The story is that I go to shul feeling disconnected, and while I might have moments of connection in the davening, for the most part I stay disconnected the whole time. I might just not care to have *kavanah*, or I might fight and fight and lose — because it is my ego that is fighting for its independence, not my soul that is fighting to be at one with Hashem.

Stories similar to the latter are way more numerous than those similar to the former.

And this is my point.

Kavanah, like everything in life, is not ours to command; it is a gift from Hashem. And if we are humble, He might give us that gift. If, however, our ego is driving us, or if we just don't care, it is highly unlikely that He will.

Kavanah is passive, not active. It's not something you work on, that you fight for; it's not something that you make happen for yourself. It's something that you open yourself up to and hope that Hashem graciously allows you to have it. And if He does not, that's His prerogative and it's fine too.

Imagine diving to the bottom of a lake to find a ring that has fallen in. As you feel around, some silt is disturbed and you can no longer see. "Fighting" for *kavanah* is like fighting the silt to go back down again. It's counterproductive. The more you fight, the more silt gets thrown up. The best thing you can do is get out of the lake, relax, and wait for the silt to settle. Then go back in calmly and see what happens this time. You might disturb the silt again, but going in calmly means that you also might not. It's still in Hashem's hands, of course, but it's your best bet.

So, what do you do to have *kavanah*? You do nothing. You just want it, and "In the way a person wants to go, so he is led."[38] Once we show the desire, the want, and we stop thinking it's we who are doing the "leading," we allow ourselves to be led. And I promise you there will be many, many times when Hashem will lead you to that precious gift of feeling a deep and meaningful connection to Him.

As with me in the story above, when I stopped disturbing the silt, the silt settled . . . and the waters of the lake were crystal clear.

---

38. *Makkos* 10b.

Chapter 3
Modes of Prayer

  The Rabbis talk in one place about ten modes of prayer,[39] and in another Medrash, they talk of thirteen.[40] In other places, they mention modes that are not covered in these first lists (such as *sichah*, which I have already mentioned and will expand upon below). There are many ways and means through which we can express our prayers. In fact, there are likely as many modes of prayer as there are human beings, because each of us is unique and each of us expresses him- or herself in his or her or her own way. But there are commonalities in what we do, and the Rabbis have categorized some of these ways in order to help us understand the potential of personal prayer.

  In the following section, I will talk about seven of these modes, the ones that I relate to the best. They should serve as guides to finding your own modes of prayer. Finding your own way of expressing your sincerity before Hashem and relating to Him is crucial; this list can be used to set

---

39. *Medrash Rabbah, Va'eschanan* 2:1
40. *Yalkut Shimoni* 811

you in the right direction. When you are able to find your own modes, you will have the keys to your own personal sincerity and connection to Hashem.

Sichah — Conversation

This is the basic mode of prayer that I have been talking about until now. Talking to Hashem. Discussing the issue. Coming to an understanding of what it means to you and what you think He expects from you. Asking Him to see you are serious and to help you understand how to change in the way He wants you to.

This is the standard, common approach to prayer. It seems to me that this is the mode to use unless you have a reason not to, for example:

    a. You are feeling frustrated with it.

    b. You feel very connected to another mode at a particular time or in a particular circumstance.

    c. You feel that a more drastic mode of prayer is required.

It's interesting to note that "conversation" is a two-way concept. In a normal conversation I talk, then you respond, then I talk more, you respond further, etc.

But how can one have a conversation with Hashem if He is not responding directly?

When we stand before Hashem in silent meditation and ask Him for what we need, answers start to come to us as to why He is not responding. Perhaps we are not doing enough; perhaps we are not serious enough; perhaps we don't care enough. If Hashem does not respond, He has a reason, and more often than not, if we are honest with ourselves, we can have a good sense of what that reason might be. It's a matter of asking, then seeing what feels wrong with how we are asking, and then trying again. This can be a back-and-forth process. We ask, we try to understand how Hashem might respond to how we're asking, and then we try again.

In effect, Hashem is communicating with us, albeit not directly. We are throwing out questions, and answers are coming our way from a deeper part of our being. Hashem speaks back to us through the medium of our own Godly soul.

Tachnunim — Begging

Children know how to do this one very well. They just don't give up. *Please give me the candy, please, please, please. I beg of you, I'm desperate, I need the candy and can't live without it!* They simply will not take no for an answer, but they are so sweet and so desperate about it that you often acquiesce.

Please Hashem, make the girl agree to marry me. Please . . . please . . . please. I know I don't deserve it. Is it best for me or isn't it? I don't know, but I do know that I want it and it would make me feel really good. So, please.

The idea is just to keep nagging away — not asking for any reason in particular other than that we really want it.

We're not touching Hashem's emotions in a way that a child does to a parent, but we are pushing and pushing and pushing — and by doing so, we intensify our own commitment to that which we desire. And Hashem responds to commitment.

If you are going to use this one, I suggest that you try to visualize yourself as a child going before Hashem. You are His little kid and you're asking Him for something you really want in the way that a little kid would.

But beware, this mode carries a government health warning of "Be careful what you ask for as you might just get it!" In other words, with the mode of conversation mentioned above, since we are questioning and debating ourselves there is a safety net of our reaching a point where we realize that perhaps we are being rash. No such safety net exists with "begging." To some extent, you are actually switching off the rational process and simply fighting for what you want no matter what. That's fine — as long as you are certain that it is really what you do want.

However, once you are certain that this is what you want, begging Hashem is a wonderful way of communicating to Him your desire.

There is another idea associated with the word *tachnunim* which comes from the Medrash. Rashi notes that the word *tachnun* has within its root the word *chinam* — free.[41] He explains that even though righteous people could ask for things based on their merits, they don't. Rather, they ask Hashem for a free gift.

What does this mean?

Righteous people appreciate that the good they do in their lives is not for Hashem but rather for themselves. It is their pleasure to be able to dedicate themselves to Hashem's service, but they understand that ultimately, Hashem does not need servants. In fact, I would suggest that this is actually the definition of a righteous person. A "regular" person who does good deeds for Hashem is trying to gain

---

41. At the beginning of *Parashas Va'eschanan*.

favor — as evidenced by the fact that when it comes to prayer, he asks Hashem to take those good deeds into account. A righteous person, however, realizes that Hashem needs nothing from him, and consequently, good deeds are not of any value as currency in Hashem's world. They have no worth to Hashem and hence are not useful as a bartering tool. Righteous people simply do what is right because it is right, as the Rambam says, "*Oseh emes mipnei shehu emes* — He does truth because it is truth."[42] When a person lives this way, he sees no point in using his good deeds as a way of asking for something, since there is no connection between the two. One might just as well go into a store and try to pay for goods with pebbles.

This idea is consistent with the translation of "begging". Essentially you are asking for something as a completely free gift and recognizing that there is nothing you can do to "earn" it, so to speak. Accordingly, you are left in a position where the only thing you can do is rely on Hashem's mercy to provide.

Rinah — Joy

Although there are others who explain it differently, I heard from my rebbe that the concept of *rinah* is focusing on the goodness that has been done already. When you see how much Hashem has done for you already and feel uplifted as a result, it motivates you to ask for more.

Hashem, You've given me life; You've given me meaning; You've given me free will; You've given me a mind, emotions, a body. The list goes on and on. Wow. So, this job that I want to get, it's only a little bit more than I've asked for in the past. Please, just give me that little, incy, wincy bit more than You

---

42. *Teshuvah* 10:3

have given me already. I know from my life experience until now that You want to give me so, so much. So how about just helping me get this job? It's such a little thing. It's nothing for You.

A good visualization technique is to try to imagine yourself asking your father if you can borrow a dime. Don't you think he would allow you? It's nothing for him compared to the love he has for his child.

Get yourself to feel excited by thinking of all that Hashem has done for you and that what you are asking for is so insignificant compared to that. Use the excitement to push you forward into confidently asking.

Rabbi Shimshon Pincus in *Shaarei Tefillah* gives the example of someone who desperately needs a loan from the bank. He knows that if only he could get a meeting with the bank manager, he would surely understand and give it to him — but it's impossible to get an appointment. As he's sitting on the bus, a man comes and sits next to him. They start to have a conversation, and he realizes that this is the very bank manager he has been trying to meet. Imagine the joy he feels and the enthusiasm with which he is able to ask him for the loan that he needs.

So too, when we remember Whom we are talking to and all that He has done for us, all the love He has shown us, we must surely feel a sense of joy to go and ask Him for what we need. This is *rinah*.

Nipul — Throwing Oneself Down

In essence, this is the human recognition of nothingness before Hashem.

Chapter 3

I'm worthless, undeserving. But please do it anyway.

The difference between this and *tachnun* is that here we are humbling ourselves. *I am nothing and I deserve nothing. But please do it for me anyway, Hashem.* Tachnun is: *I'm your child; please have mercy and love.*

Nipul puts things in perspective, and we realize that we can only fall on our faces and beg for His kindness. It's about humility. Once we realize that we are desperate — and Hashem is the only possibility of salvation — we begin to ask with a deep sense of feeling. If we think we can do it ourselves, we are less motivated to ask, but when we put things in perspective and realize how we are entirely *not* in control, then we recognize and feel the desperate need to ask.

Personally, I think one has to be careful with this one in our generation. Of course, humility is the primary character trait describing Moshe. To feel humbled before Hashem is deeply meaningful and valuable. However, it should not be, as I find it sometimes can be, at the expense of self-esteem. It's simply visualizing Hashem and His greatness, and next to Him I am a little nothing, a speck of dust in His massive universe. But there is the flip side that as a part of His universe, my life is meaningful beyond imagination and I have the potential to be great beyond measure. So, it's a balance between "I'm nothing in the face of Hashem's greatness" and at the same time "with Hashem on my side — which He most certainly is — I can be great beyond measure."

If doing this, however, will in any way play games with how you feel about yourself, then I suggest keeping well away. It's not worth damaging your level of appreciation of Hashem's love for you for the sake of slightly more meaningful prayer.

Naakah — Sighing in Desperation

Naakah is focused on how helpless we are vis-à-vis Hashem. All the power is in His hands. We have no control at all. *Naakah* is focused on the particular situation and how helpless we are in the circumstance. Obviously, it requires the right circumstance and the right feeling of helplessness. It would usually be a situation in which we have tried various means — we've prayed in various different modes; we've tried to change things; we've asked for help from others — but nothing seems to be working, and we are feeling at wits' end.

Hashem, hasn't this exile for the Jewish people gone on long enough? Look at what we've been through — inquisitions, pogroms, the Holocaust . . . And now, wars and terrorism in Eretz Yisrael. Haven't enough Jews died? Assimilation. Haven't we lost tens of millions already? When will this end; what are we to do? It all seems so hopeless . . . I feel so lost, so confused, in so much pain . . . so desperate . . . Please help us.

Indeed, this was the mode of prayer that Hashem listened to when the Jews were enslaved in Egypt, as the verse states, "*Vayishma Elo-him es naakasam* — And Hashem heard their desperate sighs."[43]

The more intense the feelings of helplessness, of confusion, of not knowing where to turn, of wanting just to curl up on the floor and cry, the more we can use the feeling of the moment to focus the prayer.

It's not so much a matter of trying to get ourselves to feel helpless. We can't get ourselves to *feel* helpless if, at the end of the day, we don't, or the circumstance does not

---

43. *Shemos* 2:24

warrant it. Instead, this is a matter of taking advantage of the feeling we are in and using the right mode of prayer as a result. For all of us, there are times in life when we genuinely feel desperate. We see no way out. This mode of prayer is simply taking advantage of the desperation and, instead of it making us give up, having it point us toward Hashem.

In a sense, it would be a shame to try to have a conversation with Hashem (*sichah*) at a time when we feel completely desperate.

Use the leverage of your desperation to cry out to Hashem and connect directly in the raw and visceral way that is available at such a time.

Tzaakah — Crying Out in Desperation

This is similar to the previous one, only it is crying out instead of sighing. It is used mostly when one is in a desperate and immediate situation of trouble. Moshe used this one at the Yam Suf after the Jews had left Egypt. The mighty Egyptian army was closing in on them from behind, and in front of them was an impassable sea. The situation was desperate, and Moshe cried to Hashem from that place of desperation. The feeling is like what we would experience if we have fallen off the edge of a cliff, and the ledge we have managed to hang onto is crumbling away. People are above us with a rope, but don't know we are there. We scream at the top of our lungs, "Heeeeeeeeeelp! Heeeeeeeeelp!!!"

Things are bad, we look up to Hashem, and, figuratively, we scream.

Although actual screaming would probably be more powerful, people around you might think you are a little strange. Maybe if you are stuck somewhere in the middle of the Antarctic with no one for miles around, you can give a try at actually screaming to Hashem and see how it feels. (And once He's saved you, please come back and tell me because I'm interested to know!) For the minute, though, and in most situations, it might be wise to stick to the silent scream.

The difference between this and *naakah* is that *naakah* has some articulation — it's a sigh. We know what we want, and we can express it to Hashem. *Tzaakah*, on the other hand, is a deeper, more primordial level. It is a purer expression of pain. It's beyond a physical expression.

My most powerful experience of *tzaakah* was when my late wife passed away. I went to pick up my three-year-old from a neighbor and told her that her mummy had gone to Hashem and she would not see her again until Moshiach came. She didn't quite get it, for obvious reasons, and on the way home, she said she wanted to see Mummy. For the previous six weeks, my wife had been in our living room with a full-time nurse, hospital bed, and all sorts of medical equipment. By the time we got there, everything was gone and the room was empty. My daughter was completely disoriented by what she saw. I took her into our back garden and we sat together on a log. We sat for a few minutes and suddenly, she let out a scream that was the most shocking sound I have ever heard in my life. It was pure and honest and unadulterated, and I recall having certainty in my heart that her scream went straight to Heaven.

This is *tzaakah* — the soul crying out to its Maker. No articulation is necessary; it's purely the feeling that matters.

Like *naakah*, this experience cannot be artificially created. If I asked my daughter now to scream that way again, it would be impossible. Moshe could not have cried out to Hashem without the Egyptians bearing down on the Jewish people. It is the feeling of desperation, combined with a person actively directing that feeling toward Hashem, that creates this most powerful mode of prayer.

Rav Pincus quotes the *Zohar* as saying that with *tzaakah*, you "never return empty-handed."

At the right time and in the right place, this mode is the most powerful of all.

Milchamah — War[44]

Unlike all the previous ones, "battle" is not a word one would naturally associate with prayer. Yet, it is perhaps the most powerful and significant of all methods. But, like all powerful things, it must be used at the right time, under the right circumstances, and with extreme caution. To put this in a crude way, it would be a strategic mistake to fire nuclear missiles when attacked by a few terrorists with knives.

In short, this mode of prayer is going to battle with Hashem. It is a bluff, of course. You can't actually fight with Hashem. But you are showing how much you care about something by being ready to stand up against Hashem Himself in order to insist that it happen. But you must mean it when you insist that you will not take no for an answer.

We see at least two examples of this mode of prayer in the Torah. Avraham insisted that Hashem save Sodom if

---

44. Although this is not one of the ten or even the thirteen expressions of prayer, we do find the word *milchamah* used in regard to prayer. The *Medrash Rabbah, Bereishis* 49:8 says, "'And Avraham drew close' (referring to Avraham's prayer on behalf of Sodom) — Rebbi Yehudah says, 'He drew close for war.'"

there was only a handful of righteous men. "The One Who judges the whole world will not do justice?[45]" contended Avraham. He was quite literally arguing with Hashem. He did it respectfully — but forcefully nonetheless.

Similarly, Moshe, after the incident of the Golden Calf, insisted that if Hashem was to destroy the Jewish people, then He must wipe Moshe out also — from both this world and the next, according to the *Zohar*[46]. In essence, Moshe said, "I want nothing to do with a God that would destroy the entire Jewish nation." This is as bold and brave a statement as one can possibly imagine. Moshe was willing to risk his entire reward in the World to Come in order to save the Jewish people. Of course, once again, he was "bluffing." He was showing Hashem how much he cared about the Jewish people, using this mechanism to do so.

Fighting for what we believe in, even with Hashem Himself, is one of the most powerful forms of prayer, because we are standing up for what we believe in. We are standing up for truth and sticking with it, even against Hashem Himself, as it were.

The idea is not that we think Hashem is wrong, of course. He is Hashem, and so He is never wrong. It's just that, as I have said before, Hashem not only allows room for us to be partners with Him, He encourages it. The introduction to Avraham's conversation with Hashem about Sodom is Hashem saying, "Could I possibly conceal from Avraham what I am about to do?"[47] Hashem wants us to take responsibility for the world as we see it, to care about His world, to be committed to His world, to "develop it and

---

45. *Bereishis* 18:25
46. *Zohar Chadash Breishis* 15a
47. Ibid. 18:17

to take care of it."[48] Even to the extent of disagreeing with Him.

Let me give a metaphor for this that might be helpful:

Let's say (hypothetically of course) that one of my children is cruel to the other. I sit down with the victim and say to him, "I'm sorry you got hurt, and I'm going to punish your brother for what he did." I will not be happy if he says, "OK, great, I want to see him suffer!" or even, "If you think that's the right thing to do, Abba, then go for it." I would hope that he might say to me that he does not want me to punish his brother and perhaps even argue on his behalf. It's not that I was going to do something and changed my mind. It's that I was going to do it even though I didn't want to do it (because no parent likes punishing his child), but I wanted to give him the chance to stand up for what he thought was right, the opportunity to protect his brother (which I would have allowed for the greater good).

So too with Hashem. He said to Moshe, "Allow me . . . and I will destroy them (the Jewish people)."[49] Hashem did not want to do it. But He gave Moshe the chance to show that he cared and to fight on their behalf.

Rabbi Weinberg told me numerous times that this mode of prayer must be used with extreme caution. We Jews fight only as an absolute last resort, when there is just no other way. We see that Avraham was very careful when using this form of prayer. He said at one point, "Please don't get angry, but . . ."[50]

---

48. Ibid. 2:15
49. *Shemos* 32:10
50. *Bereishis* 18:30

The word *Yisrael*, the name given to Yaakov, which we, his physical and spiritual descendants, have inherited, means "the one who struggles with Hashem."[51]

Milchamah is a trademark of the Jewish people. It's incredibly empowering to think that we can battle with Hashem Himself for what we believe to be true and just. Of course, Hashem knows what is true and just, and we are not going to change His mind. But, as with all prayer, the self-clarification is for our own benefit. Standing up to Hashem, as it were, develops and intensifies our own care and commitment — which is one of the fundamental components of prayer in the first place.

As a further note of caution, it would seem to me that this mode of prayer is reserved for communal matters — bigger issues, as with Avraham and Moshe — not personal problems. This is about getting upset about a seeming "injustice" that Hashem is doing or about to do. Of course, Hashem is just and would never not be. But we are always interacting with Hashem from the world as we see it. As I said before, Avraham said, "The One Who judges the whole world will not do justice?' Of course, Avraham knew, as clear as day, that the answer to that question is no. But he didn't see an actualization of that justice, and hence he was arguing that the way it looked over here, justice was not being done. Given that this is the case, it's harder to get upset and fight about the seeming "injustice" of what Hashem is doing to an individual — and most certainly if that individual is yourself! We can feel strongly about what is happening to a nation, and in particular the Jewish nation, but I think it's hard to feel quite that strongly about a single person. Nevertheless, I don't think it's impossible

---

51. Ibid. 32:29

if one genuinely and deeply cares about another human being to pray as follows from a heartfelt and sincere place:

Hashem, please don't get upset, I'm only trying to do what I think is right. I only say this because I genuinely care, but it just makes no sense to me. Why are You making this person sick? I know that You are just, and yet it feels so wrong. It feels so unfair. He is a good person. Surely he deserves better than this? He is generous. He gives to the community. What will people think if this person dies? Won't it turn people away from You? You didn't create a world for people to be distant from You. This situation just does not feel right, Hashem, and if it's not right, please, You need to change it.

Practical Suggestion

As an idea for becoming a little more comfortable with these different modes of prayer, why not try to put a small amount of time aside over the next few days or weeks and try them out one by one in various areas you might be praying for? Practice makes perfect. It's always a good idea to be well-practiced in all of the modes so that when you are in that foxhole, you can call upon them at will. I would say that even three focused minutes a day over a period of three to four weeks would put you in a very good position for using all of these modes whenever you need them.

Prayers That Are Not Our Own

All that I have talked about until now relates to personal prayer: standing before Hashem and asking for what you want in your own words. There was a time when this was the main mode of Jewish prayer. But the halachah is a little different today. We live in a different generation with different needs.

Until 2,500 years ago, the Jewish people had no siddur, no formal prayer service. Jews knew what and how to pray and did so in their own words at their own leisure.[52] Prayer should come from within, and during that period of Jewish history, it very much did so.

But there is a problem with prayer that comes from within. It requires incredible skill to be able to fully concentrate one's emotions on what one is saying while at the same time using one's mind to formulate the right words to express the ideas. To consider doing this today would be almost impossible. We need first to formulate ideas, and then work toward feeling them. Doing both simultaneously is way beyond our pay grade.

Because of this decline in man's ability, our Sages took the step of composing standardized prayers. It was done with a heavy heart, to be sure, for what one gains in clarity, one loses in rigidity and formalization.

Nowadays, we have more formalized prayer; we have a format and set prayer text created for us by the genius and Divinely inspired Anshei Knesses HaGedolah, which included prophets who communicated directly with Hashem.

However, I find that for many people, much of prayer seems to consist of standing before Hashem and asking for something that they may not feel is actually missing from their lives and asking for it in someone else's words.

---

52. There is an opinion in *Brachos* 26b that says the three daily services were instituted by the Avos, but this is more likely to mean that they did it for themselves, and when the Anshei Knesses HaGedolah instituted services, they did so in the form of the prayers of the Avos. However, even if there were three services a day prior to the Anshei Knesses HaGedolah, nevertheless, the form of the prayers themselves was completely personal.

Even for those who understand the Hebrew that they are saying, this is much harder to relate to than saying their own prayers in their own words for things that genuinely matter to them.

In this section, I hope to show that prayer that is structured can form a very powerful springboard to personal prayer — which is what the Rabbis had in mind when they wrote it.

One of the abiding legacies the Anshei Knesses HaGedolah left for the Jewish people is the prayer, or rather prayers, we call *Shemoneh Esrei*. It was to be the key medium through which the Jewish people would fulfill their daily mitzvah of prayer. Every service is centered around it. It is modified for Shabbos and Festivals, but its structure remains the same. Of all that the Anshei Knesses HaGedolah composed, this surely was their greatest accomplishment.

It is a structure through which one can develop intent and then ask for all that he could possibly want on the most personal of levels.

In order to maintain the personal nature of prayer, the Anshei Knesses HaGedolah used two techniques. Both can be seen most clearly in *Shemoneh Esrei*:

1. They created a service that is a very general structure and left it up to each individual to fill in the gaps.
2. They focused on the needs and yearnings that are common to each and every Jew, in every time and in every place, until the final redemption, after which the prayer service will, of course, need to be changed.

As we talk more about the details of *Shemoneh Esrei*, I will explain how this works.

To Use a Siddur or Not?

As with so many things in Judaism, there is no black and white answer to this question. Someone who tells you that you "must" pray from a siddur is just as right as someone who says that you "must" close your eyes and concentrate.

Personally, I prefer to close my eyes rather than look in a siddur. In fact, I would not dream of doing it any other way. But that's my thing, and it would be irresponsible of me to insist that someone else should do the same.

Nevertheless, many halachic sources urge people to pray from a siddur. The reason for this is clear. Look around in shuls and you will find a lot of people saying prayers that mean very little to them. Saying these prayers without a siddur means they can speed up, skip words, mumble, and generally disrespect the form of prayer that the Rabbis created for us. Reading from a siddur at least keeps some semblance of decorum. Hopefully, it will slow them down and help them say the words properly and respectfully. In addition, having a translation at hand often helps to permit additional focus even for those who understand Hebrew.

Additionally, when a person prays without a siddur but with his eyes open, that can create the most distracted situation of all. Glancing around the room while supposedly talking to Hashem is nothing less than farcical.

However, I think that the coin has another side. For some people, feeling deeply connected in prayer can only happen when they close their eyes. At least this is the case for me! The material world is a distraction — eyes in particular. For many, connecting to Hashem while having their eyes open to a distracting world, even if they are intently focused on a siddur, is challenging.

Of course, this whole debate is predicated on the assumption that one knows the prayers by heart. If one does not, there is no debate. There is simply no way for such a person to pray without the aid of a siddur.

I would not suggest that someone actively memorize *Shemoneh Esrei*. But like anything that one says on a regular basis, it will naturally start to be remembered over a period of time.

Saying One's Own Prayers

The fact that we have set prayers is no substitute, however, for saying our own personal prayers. In fact, quite the opposite. As I have mentioned, *Shemoneh Esrei* is merely a structure, or segue, into one's own personal experience. It is, so to speak, a house in which one prays — but not the essence of prayer itself.

I will talk about the form and content that a prayer will generally take and then explain how exactly one can accomplish this within the structure of *Shemoneh Esrei* itself.

Chapter 4
Shemoneh Esrei

It must have been a daunting responsibility for the Anshei Knesses HaGedolah to compose a prayer that, over thousands of years, every Jew would pray three times a day. We cannot begin to imagine the trepidation with which they must have approached such a task.

The first and most obvious element was the structure of this prayer. Fortunately, that was something that was already decided for them. The Oral Tradition tells us that prayer consists of three parts, in this order:

1. Praise
2. Request
3. Thanks

First, we praise Hashem, then we ask Him for what we want, and then we express gratitude for what we already have been given, including the opportunity to ask in the first place!

— Chapter 4 —

Shemoneh Esrei follows this structure. During the week it consists of nineteen blessings: three blessings of praise, thirteen blessings of request, and three blessings of thanks.

On Shabbos and Yom Tov, *Shemoneh Esrei* consists of seven blessings: three blessings of praise, one blessing of request, and three blessings of thanks.

The blessings of praise and thanks always remain the same. The requests change depending on the day. The reason for this is straightforward. Praises of Hashem are always the same. What we owe Him is always the same. At different times, however, we ask for different things.[53]

Why, indeed, did the Torah prescribe this structure of prayer?

Why Praise and Thank Hashem When We Pray?

The Gemara tells us, "Prayer is request."[54] The essence of prayer is to ask Hashem for something — not to praise Him or to thank Him. Those are both important activities, but they are not "prayer." Prayer is when one asks Hashem for something. Though we praise Him before we do so and thank Him afterward for reasons that I will now explain, the "prayer" itself is the request part.

At first glance, it might seem a little bit disrespectful to praise Hashem before we ask for something. Any parent whose child suddenly comes up to him telling him how wonderful he is, how nice a parent he is, how generous he

---

53. On Shabbos and Yom Tov, for example, because our focus is entirely on the spiritual, we move away from asking for our material needs and only ask for those needs that are spiritual in nature.

54. *Brachos* 31a

is, knows exactly what is coming next. *How long does he want the car for?*

It doesn't seem nice to tell Hashem how wonderful He is and then ask Him for our needs. It also seems futile. Hashem, after all, knows what is in our hearts.

This conclusion is based on a misunderstanding of *why* we are praising Hashem.

Much of our day-to-day life is mundane — sleeping, eating, walking, bathing . . . It's difficult to focus on Hashem and the spiritual world while engaged in such mundane activities. One cannot possibly go from a night's sleep to washing his hands and face to tending to his body's needs to showering and then to asking Hashem for what he needs with the appropriate frame of mind. We need time to refocus, time to reconnect with Hashem before we ask Him for our needs.

The purpose of praising Hashem before we make any requests is to remind ourselves Whom we are talking to, to take a moment to experience Hashem's presence and feel Him with us. Only after this reality check is it fitting to make requests.

There is another aspect also.

Imagine you are about to go in to Bill Gates to ask him for some financial help. Before you go, you take out the balance sheet for Microsoft, as well as one with his personal financial details. Bamboozled by all the zeros, you realize that what you are asking for is nothing for him. Of course he can give it to you. But does he want to?

You pull out the love letter you received from Bill (who happens to be your dad!) last week that tells you how much he loves you, how much he cares, how he will do anything for you at any time.

But maybe he's upset with you right now? You read on and see the part that talks about his love being unconditional. It doesn't matter what you do. He'll be there for you.

Wow. You burst through the door, excited to ask.

Similarly, if we use the praises correctly, they should lift us to a point where we are ready to excitedly burst through the doors of Heaven and ask Hashem for whatever we need.

Why do we thank Him afterward?

We have just been through thirteen requests that cover all areas of life. We have spent some intense moments focused on all that we do not have, all that is lacking in our lives, all that we are missing.

It's so important to end off by refocusing: Life is good. Life is great. Life is wonderful — just the way it is. Yes, we would like more, but that does not mean that what we have is not an incredible amount of blessing.

So, we take a moment to thank Hashem. Even if He does not answer any of our prayers at this moment, life is still great and we still owe Him so much. Every moment of every single day, He is giving and giving and giving. As we reach out for more and more, we cannot allow ourselves to lose this fundamental perspective.

Explaining the Words of Prayer

Sometimes, people mix up explaining prayer with explaining Torah. It's understandable. Torah is the essence of Jewish education, and so Jewish educators are used to teaching and explaining Torah. There is a certain style that our Rabbis, through the millennia, have developed to explain the meaning of Torah. It is an exacting approach that looks for new information not only in each and every word, but in each and every letter and nuance. There is nothing superfluous in Torah. This is absolutely true with regard to what Hashem wrote and also, though obviously to a lesser extent, with regard to what our Rabbis wrote.

However, I believe it is a mistake to carry this approach over to the explanation of prayer.

Unlike the goal of Torah, prayer is not there to teach us ideas about life. Its purpose is not to provide wisdom — though it is full of wisdom, of course. Its purpose is more practical than that: to provide a medium through which we human beings can have an experience with Hashem.

Words are not superfluous in prayer — but not for the same reason that they are not superfluous in Torah. Each word is not necessarily teaching something new. It is aiming to contribute to the experience of relating to Hashem. As such, many words might be used to say the same thing, albeit in subtly different ways. Words may be repeated over and again — not necessarily with new information, but with different nuances of the same information — in order to intensify and deepen the experience.

In the same way that we may repeatedly express love and affection to someone we care for in order to intensify our relationship, so too, we say the same things to Hashem over and over again because, when done effectively, it enriches our experience of relationship with Him.

In the following pages, in our discussion of *Shemoneh Esrei*, I will not delve into how each word adds new ideas and concepts. I am going to explain how words deepen our sense of connection — even if they are repeats of ideas that have already been said.

In the same vein, I will not be looking to explain what the words mean exactly. I am not looking to provide

— CHAPTER 4 —

intellectual explanations as to the meaning of the words of prayer and their significance. I will simply be providing ideas that might be helpful for people to experience greater connection through their prayers.

The words and concepts of *Shemoneh Esrei* are extraordinarily deep and profound, and I know very little of them in the grand scale of things. I will therefore not attempt to explain how each and every word in *Shemoneh Esrei* is there to offer a deeper connection. What I am aiming to do is to give a sense of connection where I am able, and not attempt to suggest anything where I feel I am not. Yet, I am hopeful that this will aid the reader in developing his own words and connection with Hashem through my experience of prayer.

Therefore, with regard to my ideas and suggestions, please remember that prayer is meant to be personal. My goal is to help move it in that direction. My goal is *not* to add to the already large body of structure associated with prayer. The Anshei Knesses HaGedolah did plenty of that.

And as a final word of warning: *please* do not just use my ideas and practical suggestions. They are ideas that are helpful and work for me. Because they are personal ideas and concepts that resonate with me, by definition, they are *not* the best ideas for you! They might be useful and helpful, but they are not what your prayers really need. What your prayers need are your own ideas, your own understanding, your own connection to the words and concepts. I provide mine in the hope that they will give you direction and impetus to do that for yourself. There is no greater way for you to improve your intent and connection in *Shemoneh Esrei* than to personalize it and make it your own. I cannot urge you strongly enough to do this. My goal is for you to get the hang of it by seeing what I do — then to go out and do it for yourself.

THE WEEKDAY SHEMONEH ESREI

As I mentioned, *Shemoneh Esrei* starts with the three blessings of praise. I will discuss what they mean and how to try to feel while experiencing them.

I was going to restrict my commentary only to words and phrases that I connect to personally. However, my editor pushed me very hard, almost to the point of insistence, to say something for every word and phrase, at least in the first three blessings. And I'm very glad that he did. In doing so, I have found new meaning in phrases that previously I felt very little connection to while saying. So the first person for whom this book has helped pray with more *kavanah* is me! I hope that there will be many more to follow.

THE THREE STEPS

First things first. We begin by taking three steps into *Shemoneh Esrei*. The idea of these three steps is to step out of the mundane world we have been living in and step into a new dimension. Step into Hashem, so to speak.

There is no need to start *Shemoneh Esrei* immediately after these three steps. In fact, it might be better to take a moment to reflect, to focus on moving to a new plane of experience.

Visualization

I try to imagine a massive door slowly opening to a large room, and I am taking three steps into that room. The room is so large that I cannot see its ceiling or walls. It is full of bright light, nothing else. I can see nothing distinct, but I know that this is the throne room of Hashem's palace, so to speak, and I feel His presence there. This visualization always gives me a great feeling from which to launch into *Shemoneh Esrei*.

Practical Suggestion

I am going to give a lot of ideas about how to focus and direct your attention during *Shemoneh Esrei*. When I took the wheel of a car for the first time, it seemed impossible. I had to steer, accelerate, brake, look at what was going on on the road, indicate an oncoming turn . . . and if it was raining (and I learned to drive in England, so there was a good chance of this), I had to turn on the wipers. I had to do this all simultaneously while aware that even one mistake could have dire consequences. I felt completely overwhelmed. However, after a few years driving, I could be driving in a storm, concentrating on my GPS, looking around, drinking a can of Coke, and talking on the phone (using a hands-free device, of course), with no problem.

New experiences are always daunting and often feel overwhelming. If one is not yet somewhat proficient at thinking through prayer, then implementing the suggestions in this book might be also. There are times when all of us are distracted, times we are frustrated, times we are unmotivated. And during those times, our prayers might not be that great. In fact, it is possible that those are precisely the times when the original halachah would have told us not to pray[55]. But the *Shulchan Aruch* represents the halachic directives taken on by the Jewish people, and we are obliged to follow its guidance and pray even when we feel nothing. Minimally, one should have *kavanah* for the first blessing, but, halachically speaking, even if one knows he will not, he should still say *Shemoneh Esrei*.[56] Of course, this is not an excuse not to try. It just means that at those times when, because we are fallible human beings, we don't have the strength and commitment to push away the distractions, we should say the words of *Shemoneh Esrei* nevertheless.

My suggestion is that, if you are looking to improve *kavanah* in *Shemoneh Esrei* (which I assume you are if you are reading this book!), you do so a little bit at a time. Try to focus on one of the blessings first, or even half of one of the blessings, or even a few words. You won't be able to do it all at once, but don't allow that to become an excuse not to start slowly and build. Judaism is not all or nothing. Any word that you say with intent and any moment of focus is a success because it is a moment of giving Hashem your heart, of connecting to Him — and any time you connect to Hashem, you are building your relationship with Him.

When I first began focusing on having *kavanah* in my *Shemoneh Esrei*, I started with a few words of the first blessing. Now, on a good day, I find myself able to focus intently on seven to eight of the blessings. And I'm still building.

Slowly but surely wins the race. Overwhelm yourself with too much and you may end up gaining nothing at all.

---

55. *Shulchan Aruch* 98:2
56. *Biur Halachah* 101, "V'im."

— CHAPTER 4 —

THE BLESSING OF OUR FATHERS

Rabbi Weinberg explained to me that the first three blessings focus on three different aspects of Hashem: Creator, Sustainer, and Supervisor. These are the three elements that form the core Jewish definition of monotheism.[57] I will talk about each blessing in general first and then go into details of what the words mean.

THE CREATOR

Creation implies purpose. The purpose of our creation specifically is kindness.[58] We are Hashem's "children," and He is our "Father in Heaven." Just as a parent's goal is to bestow kindness on his children,[59] so too, Hashem's purpose is to bestow kindness on us, His children. The first blessing focuses, therefore, on the fact that Hashem loves us and we have an ongoing relationship with him.

בָּרוּךְ, "BLESSED"

This word will be appearing again and again, so I want to make sure there is a good feeling for what this means.

When we say that someone is "blessed" in the context of human beings, we usually mean he is very fortunate.

---

57. See Ramchal, *Maamar Halkarim*, chap. 1.
58. *Tehillim* 89:3; see *Malbim*, ibid.
59. Even if this goal is not at the forefront of each parent's mind, it is the subconscious drive that pushes us to have children. Ask pretty much any half-decent parent what he wants from his children, and "that they be happy" will be one of the first things he responds.

What a lucky guy you are to have such a lovely house! You are very blessed.

Obviously, that's not what we mean when we apply the same word to Hashem.

Rabbeinu Bechaya says that the word "blessing" means "plenty and abundance."[60]

The form we are using is adjectival. It indicates a state of being as opposed to doing. Hashem *is baruch*. He *is* abundance itself, the source of all of our abundance. It is not that Hashem actively makes goodness and sends it our way. Rather, Hashem Himself is the goodness that is constantly coming our way. The goodness is Him, and that Him is abundantly coming at us, 24/7.

Specifically, however, I try to focus, as I say this word, on the fact that it is coming in *my* direction. Hence *"baruch"* means to say that Hashem is pure and abundant goodness that is coming right at me, right now.

Visualization

I try to visualize a never-ending, fast-flowing stream of blessing that is rushing from somewhere out in the cosmos, directly toward me. It's very much an approximation, but when it comes to relating to Hashem, approximations are the best we can do.

It's worth trying to feel Hashem's blessing bombarding you as you say this word. A feeling of being overwhelmed would be appropriate — not a negative feeling of overwhelmed as in being unable to cope, but a positive feeling of being unable to absorb the level of goodness that is coming your way. This is a feeling of excitement and relaxation at

---

60. *Kad HaKemach*, chap. 2.

the same time that Someone so big and powerful is taking care of me and the entire world.

Bowing

As we say the first three words of this first blessing, we bend our knees and bow. The concept is that as we start our praises of Hashem, we bow before him physically as well as with words. Specifically, we bend our knees upon saying the word *baruch*,[61] hopefully as a response — the overwhelming feeling of Hashem's blessing makes us weak at the knees. However, while the chronology is usually the emotion and then the physical response (people feel sad and then cry, not vice versa), mimicking the physical response can also help with the feeling. Hence, by making our knees as though they are weak, we can more easily experience the feeling of being overwhelmed by Hashem's blessing. We then bend the back itself at the word "*Attah* — You."[62] This is an act of humbling oneself at the first mention of Hashem — albeit even if only in pronoun form. One stands straight again when saying Hashem's Name.[63]

We bow four times during *Shemoneh Esrei*. The halachah is that one should stretch every vertebra in the

---

61. *Shulchan Aruch* 113:7.
62. Ibid.
63. Ibid; *Mishnah Berurah* 13. Given the verse the *Mishnah Berurah* quotes, it seems that one stands up during the process of saying Hashem's Name — i.e., that Hashem is the one who enables the process of standing. I have heard it said that one should stand straight and then say Hashem's Name so as not to say it while bending, but the *Mishnah Berurah* does not seem to follow this. To say Hashem's Name while bowing is an act of humility, not disrespect. As we say in the *Mussaf* service on Yom Kippur, "When the people heard the *Kohen Gadol* pronounce Hashem's Name . . . they would prostrate themselves."

spine.[64] That would not mean a straight bow, rather, one in which the back curves as much as possible, including the neck. The *Mishnah Berurah* says that each vertebra should protrude from the skin.[65] If one is not flexible enough to do that, he should bend to the best of his ability.

Bowing in this way is an opportunity to humble oneself before Hashem and feel connected. I find that I get a lot out of bowing and holding my bow for a few seconds as I take in the moment.[66] I am submitting myself to my Creator. It can be hard to feel the magnitude of that without a moment or two to reflect. I highly recommend taking the time to do this. The Rabbis gave us words and actions in *Shemoneh Esrei* as a means of guiding us to a deeper connection. It's a shame to go through the motions, doing quick bows, and not reap the rewards.

אַתָּה, "You"

This is an amazing word, and it says so much about the nature of what we are doing in prayer. We are not talking in theory, in the third person, about some distant Being. We are not describing or discussing something hypothetical. This is the second person — *You*. You, Hashem. Imagine Hashem's presence right before you. He is here in the room with you, in front of you, listening to your every word. There is a sense of intimacy. Try to put the whole world to one side and imagine that there is nothing in this moment but you and Hashem.

---

64. *Orach Chaim* 117:4
65. Ibid, *se'if katan* 10.
66. See *Brachos* 12a, which says one should be quick to bow and slow to come up, as an act of submission.

Chapter 4

י-ה-ו-ה, "Ado-nay"

There are many Names that we use for Hashem, but the Names י-ה-ו-ה and the next one, *Elo-heinu*, are the main ones used in prayer.

By definition, whenever we do so much as think of Hashem, let alone think of a word to describe Him, we are minimizing Him and anthropomorphizing Him. To confine Him to the finite space of our little mind is to make Him less than what He is. We are taking the Infinite and describing it in finite terms by the mere fact of thinking about it or associating terminology to describe Him.

The only way we can describe Hashem is though *our* perception of Him, not through His actual essence. When we refer to Hashem as "Hashem," it literally means "The Name" because this is the concept of a name. A name is the way we relate to someone; it does not necessarily describe who they actually are.

So this first Name, י-ה-ו-ה, has two aspects to it. It is not pronounced the way it is written. This is because the written form of this Name is such a deep and powerful understanding of Hashem that without the confines of the Beis HaMikdash, we no longer pronounce it. It has to be said with meaning, feeling, understanding, and purity, or not said at all. You can see why for thousands of years the Jewish people have chosen to use this Name and why that choice has nowadays become halachah.

To look at its written form first, the four letters are a composite of three words: היה, "He was"; הוה, "He is"; and יהיה, "He will always be."

We take the letter י from the word היה, the ו from the word הוה, and the י and ה from the word יהיה.

This Name describes our limited understanding of Hashem as the Infinite Being. But even this, the most holy of all Names, is not a description of His infinite essence. *Infinite* in real terms does not mean "was, is, and always will be." It means completely outside of the whole dimension of time. It is a concept that cannot possibly be comprehended by man, let alone expressed in finite words, and so we do not even try.

We relate to Him, however, as a Being that spans all of time. He is the same today as He was thousands of years ago and as He will be in thousands of years. He is monolithic in the dimension of time. Unchanging.

Infinite also implies nonspatial. He does not stretch on forever. Just like He is outside of the dimension of time, He is also outside of the dimension of space.

The finite world exists within Hashem's infinite essence. To use an analogy, it is like a world that you create in your mind. You see trees; you see flowers; you see people — but all are only existing within your mind. They have no real, independent, and tangible existence. So too, the finite world is just a very, very good illusion that appears to be tangible. However, it all only exists, so to speak, in Hashem's mind. If I think of a person in my mind, the minute I stop thinking of him he is gone. So too, the minute Hashem would stop "thinking about" us, we would cease to exist.

This timelessness and everything that we have discussed above is all expressed in the Ineffable Name of Hashem. We don't pronounce this Name because it's just too difficult to take in.

But it's still worth trying to feel some sense of what this is about because even a small taste of it has real power to connect us to something much deeper.

— CHAPTER 4 —

Visualization
(This one's a little more complex)

Try to imagine yourself looking at the planets of our solar system. You are looking from a distance at planets, including Earth, orbiting a massive star. Now look beyond all that and "see" Hashem. You can't "see" Him, obviously. Just try to feel Him, and as you feel Him, the solar system disappears and Hashem alone remains. The moment you "see" Hashem, you see nothing else other than Hashem. The minute you "touch" Hashem, all else fades away.

As a crude analogy, sometimes I speak to my wife on the way home from work. I continue talking to her on the phone until the minute I walk into the room and see her. The conversation continues seamlessly with the real person rather than the phone's electronic imitation of the person. The moment I see her, the voice on the phone becomes irrelevant. The phone was a representation, an echo of my wife, but once I see the real deal in three dimensions, the phone ceases to exist for me as a means of connecting to her. So too with Hashem. The minute I get an inkling of the real thing — at whatever level He allows me to grasp — the echoes cease to have meaning.

All this is with regard to the written form of the word. In terms of the lesser Name of Hashem that we use to pronounce the written one, i.e., *Ado-nay*, the Rabbis tell us to consider this Name also as we say the word.

Ado-nay means "Master of the universe." It is Hashem in the sense that He controls everything. He makes the planets move. He makes gravity attract instead of repel. He makes winds blow and rain fall. He is the "Master of ceremonies" of the universe. It's a little easier to relate to than the written form (as I've explained above), and so we pronounce it as *Ado-nay* to give us something more tangible to hold onto.

If that direction gives you more of a sense of connection when you say the word, by all means use it. If the former does, that's great too. And if you can do both at the same time, that's best of all. But in my mind, you need to be pretty proficient to do that trick, and I would recommend focusing on one or the other until you get really comfortable with it before trying to bring in something completely different.

Practical Suggestion

Ideally, one should focus on both aspects of Hashem as he says the word. I strongly suggest, however, that you start with the second (i.e., *Ado-nay* — Master of the world) and only once you are proficient, to move on to the first (י-ה-ו-ה) — Infinite Essence). The latter is much more esoteric, so I recommend going for the lower-hanging fruit first. Halachically, also, the spoken word always trumps the written word. Hence, the main intent for this word is *Ado-nay*, with י-ה-ו-ה being secondary.

אֱלֵקֵינוּ, "Our God"

This Name of Hashem implies absolute and uncompromising justice. At first glance, that might sound a little harsh. How does remembering that make us feel more connected to Him?

In human society, we have a justice system for one main purpose: to protect people from each other. It is a way to discourage following the baser human nature by providing consequences to our actions. In that sense, *justice* is not really the correct word. A *penal system* would be a more accurate description because the goal is not to mete out absolute Justice with a capital J; it is to create a stable society that we can all live in. Our "justice" system is practical, not idealistic.

Hashem, however, does not need justice in order to create a secure society. And He does not need to implement His justice as a means of control. Control is meaningless to Him. In our universe, with Hashem as the Infinite Being, His great challenge, so to speak, is how to give away control (and hence create free will), not how to command it.

Justice, then, from Hashem's perspective, is about something else. It is about Hashem providing consequences for our actions in order to make our lives meaningful. He responds to the choices that we make. As the Rabbis say, "Hashem leads us in the way that we want to go."[67] Our choices produce natural and logical conclusions. In the same way that if I play with a knife, I might cut myself — the blood would be a consequence, not a punishment — so too, my spiritual choices produce definite logical outcomes. Hashem is interacting with us moment to moment, deciding — "judging" — what is best for us based on the decisions we have made. And as we make new decisions, He is recalibrating that judgment, so to speak. It's literally unimaginable how He could possibly do such a thing considering that, as I have said above, He is outside of time, but that again is indicative of our inability to imagine anything that is touching on the infinite.

In our modern world, there is a very nice metaphor for this — a GPS system. As I make a turn that is not in line with the GPS's instructions, it recalculates – and a completely

---

67. *Makkos* 10b

new route is provided as a response to my change in direction. If I change the route again, it will recalculate again. And there is an infinite number of potential recalculations. But there is always an underlying goal that never changes: to get me to my destination. So too with Hashem, there is an unchanging, underlying goal — to guide me to the spiritual destination of connection to Him. "Justice" is the continual recalculation of that path — for better or for worse.[68]

Justice implies that He responds to our actions, that we have a relationship with Him at every possible moment. While י-ה-ו-ה implies the God Who is infinite and transcendent (and hence, perhaps one might feel, a little distant), *Elo-heinu* implies God Who is intimately involved with us at every moment. Responding and reacting.

Why? For our benefit, of course. As our Father in Heaven, He is giving us free will and trying to help us use that free will to our greatest advantage. He did not create His world and walk away; He is actively engaged in our lives and responding to us at every moment. Elo-heinu, as such, is the God of relationship.

So those are the two Names separately. The juxtaposition of the two, which we find in *Shemoneh Esrei* — י-ה-ו-ה אֱלֹקֵינוּ — adds a completely new dimension.

---

68. There is a fine balance between Hashem recalibrating the path to lead a person to a connection to Him and also Hashem leading a person in the way that he chooses. Let's say that a person wants to steal. Hashem will allow him to be in situations where he can do so. But once he has stolen, "justice" kicks in, and there will be consequences to the choice he has made. The person might respond well to those consequences and choose not to steal next time — and Hashem will then lead him in the direction of not stealing. Or he may continue to choose to steal and Hashem will continue to allow him to do so, but once again, there will be different consequences based on the different actions that he has done. It's a bit of an oversimplification, but I would say that Hashem leading a person in the way he wants to go is leading up to the action, whereas justice is post the action.

— CHAPTER 4 —

Let's consider for a moment how amazing these two words are together.

י-ה-ו-ה — the Infinite, Transcendent Being — is nevertheless *Elo-heinu*, a Being with an intimate involvement in our day-to-day lives. It is He who provides the reaction to our every action, Who recalibrates the GPS after every human being's false turn. It always boggles my mind to really think deeply about this one. That a Being Who is so above and beyond this entire universe can nevertheless care about and respond to our every action is just amazing.

אֱלֹקֵי אֲבוֹתֵינוּ, "GOD OF OUR FATHERS"

This clearly does not mean God of our forefathers Avraham, Yitzchak, and Yaakov, as the three are mentioned explicitly in the next few words. I understand it to mean that Hashem has been our God for all the generations. This relationship that we talked about above is not a fly-by-night relationship. It is not something that came about last week, or even the week before. It has been around for thousands of years, since the existence of the Jewish people. It is very, very, very solid. One cannot compare the strength of the bond in a newly married couple to that of a couple who have been married for fifty years. Imagine the strength of a marriage lasting over three thousand years!

Hashem's relationship with us is one that has stood the test of time. He is an old and loyal family Friend. He deeply loved your father, your grandfather, your great-grandfather, etc. He has been there for us throughout generations, and we can feel that we can trust Him intimately.

Rabbi Weinberg used to compare it to an old business — or a business pretending to be old, at least! "Established in 1861" sounds very impressive. It gives you the feeling that this company has been around and knows what it's doing; that it's reliable. So too with our relationship with Hashem. "Established in 1951" (years from the beginning of creation, when Avraham was three years old) might be an appropriate tagline for the relationship. The Jewish nation's relationship with Hashem is as old as that. Established, secure, constant, and everlasting.

So, I try to think back to my father, to my grandfather, to my great-grandfather, and beyond and to realize that Hashem was there for them, every single one of them, in exactly the same way as He is here for me right now. Nothing has changed. This is a long-established and stable relationship. In fact, the only reason I can even exist today is because Hashem was directly looking after my ancestors. Both of my grandfathers fought in World War I, and my father participated in D-Day in World War II. There were shells and bullets whizzing past them, and Hashem was taking care of them, ensuring that they survived and thrived. Going back further to pogroms and inquisitions, to exiles, plagues, and wars, Hashem was carefully looking after every single one of my ancestors, ensuring that I would be here today.

That's a very powerful thought for me.

CHAPTER 4

אלקֵי אַבְרָהָם אלקֵי יִצְחָק וֵאלקֵי יַעֲקֹב, "God of Avraham, God of Yitzchak, and God of Yaakov"

There seems to have been a much easier way to have made the same point. It could have just said, "God of Avraham, Yitzchak, and Yaakov." Why say "God" each time? Is this not superfluous?

Let's remember again what we are doing here. We are introducing ourselves to Hashem again, reminding *ourselves* Whom we are talking to and what our relationship with Him is like. I believe that the Anshei Knesses HaGedolah gave us here another tool for feeling the relationship.

The God I am talking directly to right now was also God to Avraham. He was also God to Yitzchak, and He was God to Yaakov. He is not older; He has not become less enthusiastic over the years; He has not developed different attitudes or changed in any way. He has not because He is infinite and unchanging. That very same God I read about with regard to Avraham is the God that I have a direct audience with right now. Wow, that's something special!

So why the "God of" each time before referring to Avraham, Yitzchak, and Yaakov? Because His relationship with each was different and unique — in the same way as each of them was unique. The God we see in His relationship with Avraham is not the same God as we see Him in His relationship with Yitzchak nor in His relationship with Yaakov. In each, we see different expressions of Who He is, different traits, different aspects of His relationship with us.

What is important to remember here is this: we are talking to Hashem, not to a wall. We need to realize that

Hashem is right here in front of us, right here inside of us. That's what we are trying to feel. We've said this already – "You, Hashem, are a wellspring, a transcendent Being Who has an intimate relationship with us . . ." Now we are reminding ourselves that this Being, this self-same Being Whom we stand before right now, is the Being Who related to Avraham with the love that He did and related to Yitzchak and to Yaakov with the same love but in different ways. He has not changed; He has not aged; He is no different in any way. This God is the same God Who related to Avraham. Not three thousand years older and more cynical — no, exactly the same as He was then, He is now. If the relationship is any different from the way it was then, it is because *we* have changed, not He. We are talking to the same Being.

Practical Suggestion

You need a little more knowledge for this one, but when I do it, which is fairly regularly, I find it to be the most helpful and connecting of all the ideas that I have discussed in the first blessing of *Shemoneh Esrei*.

אלקֵי אַבְרָהָם, "God of Avraham"

With regard to *Elo-hei Avraham*, I think of the relationship Avraham had with Hashem — it's easy to see Hashem's love and care and commitment. Hashem told Avraham, out of the blue, not to fear.[69] He knew that Avraham was worried, and He wanted to actively ease his concern. He saved him from the furnace when he was thrown in by the pagan King Nimrod[70]. Avraham walked through completely unscathed. When Avraham wanted — no, needed — to do

---

69. *Bereishis* 15:1 (see *Rashi*).
70. *Bereishis Rabah* 38:11

— CHAPTER 4 —

kindness for others, He sent angels. When Avraham was at war against a vastly superior army, all he had were dirt and stones; he threw them and Hashem turned them into arrows and spears[71]. That is relationship; that is commitment; that is love. And that exact same relationship is available for me with the exact same God. Right here, right now. Hashem wants the same relationship with me as He had with Avraham. (The question is just whether I am willing to step up to the plate in the way that Avraham did.) That's what's available to me in this section of *Shemoneh Esrei*.

אלֹקֵי יִצְחָק, **"God of Yitzchak"**

The Medrash tells us that Yitzchak went blind because the angels cried tears into his eyes at the time of his binding to be killed by Avraham.[72] Hashem, so to speak, via the angels, cried. He cried because He did not want His beautiful child Yitzchak to be killed. Hashem is a God Who cries for the pain of His children. That same God surely cries for me also. He cries for my pain.

This one I love: Yitzchak went around Eretz Yisrael digging wells, and each well was filled in by the local Philistines as an act of enmity. He was digging wells in a desert. Yet every single place that he dug a well, he found water. Isn't that just beautiful? Yitzchak dug and Hashem filled his hole with water. That's the God I am talking to. A filler of wells. If I dig wells, will He not fill them for me also? He is the same God, after all.

וֵאלֹקֵי יַעֲקֹב, **"And God of Yaakov"**

Yaakov said when he returned to Eretz Yisrael, "With my staff I crossed this Jordan River and now I am two

---

71. *Bereishis Rabah* 43:7
72. See *Rashi, Bereishis* 27:1

camps." When Yaakov had left Eretz Yisrael twenty-eight years earlier, he had left with nothing — just the staff in his hand. He returned an incredibly wealthy man with four wives and thirteen children. Hashem was there for him even in difficult times, and he prospered. I'm talking to the same God, and He is more than willing to do the same for me.

This is another of my favorites: On his way back to Eretz Yisrael, Yaakov was pursued by Lavan, the evil trickster who always portrayed himself as whiter than white. Ostensibly, he was chasing Yaakov to say goodbye to his daughters and grandchildren. But Hashem knew his intention was to kill Yaakov. So, Hashem appeared to Lavan in a dream that night. He told him, in essence, "You lay so much as a finger on Yaakov and I will kill you." How's that for love and protection and concern?

Sorry to harp on about it, but that is what we are trying to do here. There is no such thing as overkill in prayer, too much connection or too much feeling.

Hashem took away Yaakov's favorite son, Yosef. In fact, Yaakov believed him to be dead. But Hashem had something in mind. He wanted Yaakov to be great, and this was part of the plan. And in the end, Yosef returned, and Yaakov saw that it was all for a reason. Well, Hashem has a plan for me also. He is here with me also. He wants me to be great also. He is waiting to have the same relationship with me as he had with Yaakov. But it's up to *me* to have the same relationship with Him.

"הָקֵל הַגָּדוֹל הַגִּבּוֹר וְהַנּוֹרָא קֵל עֶלְיוֹן, "The Almighty One, the Great One, the Powerful One, and the Awesome One, Almighty on high"

The Gemara indicates that these words were actually instituted by Moshe himself.[73] The phrase is, indeed, a direct quote from the Torah.[74] This, in my mind, very much adds to their significance and value.[75]

הָקֵל, "The Almighty"

This refers to Hashem as the source of all energy and power in the universe. There is nothing He cannot do, and nothing happens that is not His doing.

הַגָּדוֹל, "The Great"

This refers to Hashem's greatness in the creation of our universe and all that is within it. See below for more on this.

---

73. *Yuma* 69a

74. *Devarim* 10:17

75. The Gemara says that Yirmiyah stopped saying "the awesome One" when he saw an enemy army lay waste to the Beis HaMikdash. "Where is Hashem's awe?" he asked. Daniel stopped saying "the great One" upon seeing the Jewish people enslaved by the Babylonians. "Where is Hashem's greatness?" he asked. The Gemara asks, however: If Moshe indeed instituted these words, how could Yirmiyah and Daniel stop saying them?

The answer serves to emphasize the essence of the message of this book: "Since they knew that Hashem is truthful, they did not want to speak falsely about Him." Consider this for a moment. I would imagine that both Yirmiyah and Daniel knew, in theory, that Hashem is "awesome" and "great." They did not, God forbid, doubt such foundations of Jewish faith. However, what the Gemara clearly means is that they did not at the time *feel* this way about Hashem. They knew it in theory but did not feel the truth of it because they could not see it in the world at that point in history. As such, they chose not to say the words rather than pay lip service to them. Again, this is not practical halachah, but the point remains: prayer is about meaning it, not saying the words.

הַגִּבּוֹר, **"The Mighty"**

This refers to the fact that Hashem is in constant control of anything and everything that happens in our world. Again, see below for more.

וְהַנּוֹרָא, **"And the Awesome One"**

This refers to the fact that Hashem's greatness is completely and utterly beyond human comprehension and overwhelming even to consider.

I saw an idea in the siddur *Iyun Tefillah* on the next three words that I think can lead to very helpful imagery. It says that *hagadol* refers to Hashem's creation of the world, *hagibor* refers to Him taking the Jewish people out of Egypt, and *hanora* refers to the splitting of the Yam Suf. There is a lot of potential here for considering each event as one says the words.

The great: Close your eyes and think of the incredible "sound-and-light show" that Hashem's creation of our universe must have been. One moment empty space, the next moment a planet is there. One moment an empty world, the next moment it is inhabited by billions of animals and insects. That's Hashem's greatness.

The mighty: Now consider the Exodus from Egypt. Try to picture yourself in a helicopter above it all. Two and a half million Jews simply walk out with Clouds of Glory leading the way. It gives me shivers to consider it. That's Hashem's greatness.

The Awesome One: The splitting of the Yam Suf; that simply tops it off. *Awesome* is the word and awesome is the deed. Imagine the nation standing there in complete awe as the sea splits, leaving dry land in the middle.

Once again, this is my take on it. But the words and concepts are much greater and broader than I can illustrate in a few words. Take them and find what speaks to you in them. Make them your own. And keep developing your understanding and feeling.

These words, actually, are a great example for me. Until recently, I had not related to them at all and hence said them quickly when I prayed my *Shemoneh Esrei*. I was not going to say anything about them in this book as, like Daniel and Yirmiyah in the footnote above, I don't like to say something that I don't mean. However, my publisher, Rabbi Moshe Kormornick, requested that I do some research and at least write something that others say and might be useful for people. I agreed, and so I looked up these words. I found the *Iyun Tefillah* above and incorporated it into my *Shemoneh Esrei*, and it has added a new level of meaning for me. After thirty-five years of praying *Shemoneh Esreis*, I can finally say these words with some sense of understanding.

Slowly but surely, you add more meaning to your *Shemoneh Esrei* over the years, and before you know it, you will be praying with a great deal of focus and intent.

קֵל עֶלְיוֹן, **"Almighty on high"**

The Gemara says that from the Earth to the first heaven (*rakia*) is a five hundred-year journey.[76] And the first heaven itself is a five hundred-year journey thick. Each heaven is also a five hundred-year journey from the one before it, and then the "feet" of the angels are equivalent to all the previous distances, as are the bodies, heads, and horns of the angels, the feet of the Throne of Glory, and the Throne of Glory itself. Above all of this resides the living and enduring Hashem (*Keil*). Obviously, this is metaphorical, but you get a sense of the spiritual distance between us

---

76. *Chagigah* 13a

and Hashem, the "Almighty on high." The *Yerushalmi* adds that nevertheless, a person stands in a corner and says his prayer in a whisper — and this "spiritually distant" Hashem hears every word.[77] Wow.

Visualization

Try to imagine yourself looking up further and further into the sky. Feel your soul floating upward, higher and higher and higher, above the Earth, beyond the skies, out of the atmosphere, toward the moon. See past the moon to the planets — Mars, Jupiter, Saturn . . . Higher yet to the stars of the Milky Way. And beyond to distant galaxies. Somewhere higher yet, beyond the stars even, at the edge of the physical universe . . . Try to feel Hashem's presence. Now say the words "Hashem on high," and feel the magnitude of His loftiness. Whenever I do this I can't help but shiver at the thought of it.

גּוֹמֵל חֲסָדִים טוֹבִים, "PURVEYOR OF GOOD KINDNESSES"

This seems redundant. Surely *all* kindnesses are good?

The reality is that there are two aspects of Hashem's giving to us. There is "good." This is what is objectively good for us. It is what we need to grow and develop properly, what we need to push us toward achieving our potential and becoming great human beings. It might not always *feel* so nice, but it is certainly "good" in the ultimate sense of the word. A parent might force his children to eat peas before they get chocolate. It is "good" that they eat the peas. The

---

77. *Brachos* 9:1

Chapter 4

children might not like the peas, but peas are what they need to grow healthily.

Then there is "kindness." Kindness *feels* good. It makes us feel happy. It is kind to give sweets to a child. It might not be good for the child, but it will make the child feel good in the short term.

"Good kindnesses" are circumstances in life that we grow from and at the same time make us feel good also.

But, one may say, Hashem does not always provide goodness that feels good also. We know that He is always good, that He always has our best interests in mind. But sometimes a tough response is required, and what we get in life doesn't always feel so great. For example, if someone has broken his leg, it might well be *good* for him,[78] but it certainly doesn't feel very nice.

So, let's remind ourselves again: We are not describing the world here. We are describing Hashem, Who and What He is, so to speak. We are getting in touch with the incredible essence of the Being we are appearing before. Hashem is the "purveyor of good kindnesses." That is Who He is in essence. That is part of our definition of Him. He is a Father Who is committed to doing what is right for us, and at the same time He wants the good that He is bestowing to feel good for us. In fact, He would do it always — if only His own higher desire to do what is right for us would "permit" Him to do so. Sometimes circumstances arise in which He must put us through pain. That's inevitably our responsibility because it is a response to our behavior, not what He would like to have happened if we had behaved appropriately.

---

78. For more on this, I recommend my book *Why Bad Things Don't Happen to Good People*. In short, though, something painful might come to a person as a message to change, as a means of humbling him and bringing him closer to Hashem, as an atonement, or for other reasons.

It actually goes against His nature, so to speak. When we are in pain, He suffers with us ("I am with you when you suffer"[79]). He does not want to do it, but we force His hand through our actions — or lack of them.

But let's remember, in *Shemoneh Esrei*, we are not analyzing what Hashem does and making philosophical judgments about it. This is not Torah learning. We are not looking at what He does, we are looking at Who He is, and in essence He is a purveyor of good kindnesses. That is His deep and unchangeable nature. He is eager and excited to give us goodness that feels good also. He is trying all the time to do so. He is pouring out goodness toward us, and if we allow it, that goodness will feel good also.

Remember, if there is pain in the world, He feels it more than we do. He wants it less than we do.

Try at this point to pause for a moment and feel His incredible benevolence and love.

וְקוֹנֵה הַכֹּל, "And He possesses everything"

Not only does He want to give to us and make us feel good at the same time, He also has the wherewithal to do so.

He possesses everything. It all belongs to Him. Every single atom of this entire universe is His to command. And command He does.

In your mind, go through the things you are planning on asking for and realize that each belongs to Him.

A new car? Every car is His to give. Every single one on the road, in the factory, and those that are not yet built!

---

79. *Tehillim* 91:15

Wisdom? He has it all. It all belongs to Him. In fact, more than that, He does not just "have" wisdom, He *is* wisdom itself. He is the only place to go for wisdom. He can provide as much as you want and as immediately as you want it.

Love? Love is His. Love is Him. He is the Master of every one of us. He has a perfect partner waiting for each of us. He knows where exactly he or she is and is able to put all of the pieces into place to bring you both together at any time.

There is absolutely nothing that He cannot do for you.

Combine these last two phrases and you have a powerful boost in your *Shemoneh Esrei*:

You stand before a Being Who only wants to give what is good, and only wants that giving to feel good also. That is His whole intent. And He possesses everything and anything that you could possibly need or want.

In short, Hashem is our billionaire Father, and we have a private audience with Him right now. Surely, we can get ourselves excited by that?

"And וְזוֹכֵר חַסְדֵּי אָבוֹת, He 'remembers' the kindnesses of the fathers"

Even a full appreciation of all the above, however, might leave a niggling issue that bothers us and holds us back from knowing just how much Hashem is waiting to give to us.

We might feel — incorrectly, of course — that we are not worthy of Hashem's love. Funny as that might sound, we are the low-self-esteem generation. Many of us feel we deserve nothing because we are not good enough, that we have not lived in a way that is befitting of Hashem's goodness in response. In short, we may worry that that which is good for us might end up not being that which feels good as a result of Hashem punishing us "sinners."

In response to this, *Shemoneh Esrei* reminds us that Hashem remembers the kindnesses of the forefathers. Let me explain how that works.

First, let's look at the word "remember" when associated with Hashem. Hashem, quite obviously, does not forget, and therefore, He does not need to remember. But let's look at what remembering is for a moment and see how it might apply to Hashem. When a human being remembers something that he has forgotten, it means that it comes back from the back of his mind, so to speak, to the forefront of his consciousness. Remembering means keeping something at the front of your mind. To remember something that you have completely forgotten is impossible. But to remember something that has fallen to the back of your mind by allowing it to rise to the surface of your consciousness is quite possible to do.

As always, anything we say about Hashem is anthropomorphic and metaphoric. So, when we say "remember" in association with Hashem, we mean that it is at the forefront of His mind, so to speak. It is what He focuses on and what He responds to.

So, this phrase is saying that Hashem focuses on and responds to the kindnesses of our forefathers. He keeps that at the forefront of His mind, above all else. We, and our inappropriate actions and decisions, are not at the forefront of His mind. They are further back, so to speak.[80] The kindnesses of the forefathers are what He focuses on instead.

---

80. The Rabbis tell us (see *Rashi, Bereishis* 1:1) that Hashem wanted to create the world with the attribute of judgment, but He "realized" that the world would not survive with this attribute alone, so he included the attribute of kindness also.

But what is this kindness of the fathers that Hashem is focused on?

Zechus avos — the "merit of the fathers" — is a key concept in Jewish thinking. Rabbi Weinberg explained:

If you could compare the DNA of Avraham to the DNA of one of his descendants today, you would discover that they match. DNA is the blueprint through which we pass on our character to future generations, and Avraham's blueprint, like anyone's, is passed on to his descendants even four thousand years later.

So *zechus avos* is spiritual DNA. Avraham, Yitzchak, and Yaakov made certain changes to their spiritual makeups. They made deep and fundamental alterations to who they were and how they related to Hashem and other human beings. Theirs were not just changes in action, but changes in the character of their beings. They changed their spiritual makeups and created, between the three of them, the Jewish soul.

This Jewish soul has a spiritual DNA. And that spiritual DNA is passed on to each and every Jew who descends from Avraham, Yitzchak, and Yaakov. (For a convert, that DNA is given over by Hashem when he converts, so even he has the exact same spiritual DNA that our forefathers had.) As such, there is a part of each of us that is a potential Avraham, a potential Yitzchak, and a potential Yaakov. We have it within us.

Zechus avos means that Hashem looks at that potential instead of looking at where we are at any one point. He looks at this part of us that has within it the "kindnesses"

Kindness is a delaying of judgment. Instead of immediate consequences to bad choices, Hashem holds off and gives us time to sort ourselves out instead. This is how I understand "forefront" and "back" of Hashem's mind. It is not whether He remembers or not — of course He remembers. It's a question of whether He responds immediately (forefront) or He holds off until a later date (back).

of our fathers and makes this His focus in His judgment of us. He remembers this part of us. He focuses on this aspect of who we are and responds to this no matter who or what we might have become.

In short, if we are making a spiritual mess of our lives, it doesn't mean that good — and even good that feels good — cannot come our way, because Hashem knows what we can be. He knows what we can achieve. He knows our incredible potential and will respond to us in these terms. He will respond to who we can be, not who we are. And who we can be is something quite incredible.

וּמֵבִיא גוֹאֵל לִבְנֵי בְנֵיהֶם לְמַעַן שְׁמוֹ,
"AND BRINGS A REDEEMER TO THEIR CHILDREN'S CHILDREN FOR THE SAKE OF HIS NAME"

Not only is Hashem looking after us in the day-to-day details of our lives, He has His eye on the bigger picture also. He is giving us what we need moment to moment, but also has in mind, so to speak, to bring a full and complete redemption to human suffering. Not for our sake — because if we needed to merit it, it might never happen — but for "the sake of His Name." As the last Mishnah in *Avos* says, "All that Hashem created, He only created for His honor." It is for the sake of Hashem's greatness becoming manifest in our world that He will bring the redemption. As such, there is a guarantee that it will happen — because, fortunately for us, it does not depend on us!

— Chapter 4 —

בְּאַהֲבָה, "With love"

In spite of the fact that the world achieving its ultimate goal will happen for Hashem's higher purpose, Hashem will nevertheless do it with love. He will have us in mind and ensure that we are the ultimate recipients of the world attaining its perfection.

מֶלֶךְ, "King"

The Torah sees a king as a "servant of the nation."[81] While Hashem is obviously not our servant, He reigns over us not for His own sake, but for ours — in order to provide stability, order, and progress in our lives. Children, younger ones especially, thrive on having structure in their lives. So too us. We thrive on structure — on clear rules, values, direction, and focus. With Hashem as our King, we have a structure in which we can flourish and grow.

עוֹזֵר, "Helper"

When you find ourself in trouble, Hashem is always there to lend a helping hand. When you are on the edge of a cliff, hanging on by your fingertips, it is His hand that will stretch out for you to grab. If you are struggling with exams, it's He Who can and will give you a hand to do well. If you have lost your way, it's He Who will hold your hand and guide you home.

---

81. See *Melachim I* 12:7 and *Malbim*, ibid.

מוֹשִׁיעַ, "Savior"

Moreover, not only does Hashem help us in times of trouble, He provides salvation to get us out of the trouble entirely — not just a bit of help to put us in a more tenable position. He solves the problem for us completely. Think of times you have been in real trouble, whether it was an illness, financial or legal problems, whatever it might be. And now it has passed. That was Hashem — and He will be there in the same way in the future. Indeed, He is here in the same way right now.

Practical Suggestion

I can think of many times in my life when I have been in real trouble. Once, I came within a moment of drowning when I was the only person on Herzliya Beach at 5 a.m., so no one would have pulled me out. Another time, I had a kidney stone and felt pain so intense that it took over my entire existence. I contrast these circumstances with my position now, as I stand here speaking to Hashem, alive and free of pain. That is Hashem's complete and full salvation. It's hard not to feel grateful and deeply connected when I consider these situations and others like them.

וּמָגֵן, "Shield"

Savior means that He gets us out of trouble when we are in it, but *shield* means there are many times when there is potential trouble and He simply prevents it from happening.

Years ago, in England, there was a commercial for a kids' cereal called Ready Brek. The children would eat the cereal and then start to glow. They would walk outside into a freezing winter day with the wind howling and the snow falling with an orange, glowing force field around them, as though nothing could touch them or harm them during the day as long as they had eaten their Ready Brek. I often have the image of a Ready Brek child in my mind when I say this word in *Shemoneh Esrei*. Hashem is like a glowing force field around me. I walk out in the street and nothing can touch me, nothing can harm me, because Hashem's glow is all around me. He is my shield, and whatever comes my way will simply bounce off!

בָּרוּךְ אַתָּה ה' מָגֵן אַבְרָהָם, "You are the source of all goodness, Hashem, shield of Avraham"

He is not simply a shield, but the shield of Avraham. On the one hand, this is a reminder that Hashem took care of Avraham and He will take care of me also.[82] But I think there is something deeper as well. There is a part inside every one of us that I would refer to as "Avraham," that DNA of the soul that I mentioned earlier, the holy part of ourselves that remains pure no matter what. And the reason it remains pure is because God is its shield. That soul inside each of us is looked after by God himself. He builds

---

82. I would suggest that the reason Avraham is singled out in the close of the blessing is because the sense of the "shield" that Hashem provided for Avraham would be diminished by adding Yitzchak and Yaakov. Both of them had a father to guide and look after them. Avraham took a different path from his father and, hence, was completely alone and vulnerable in the world. Therefore, Hashem's role as a shield for Avraham was so much more obvious than for Yitzchak and Yaakov.

a "Ready Brek" force field around it and no matter what, it will remain pure and unsullied.

In summary, I am completely safe as I walk through this world. God is looking after me both physically and spiritually, and, no matter what, I will be OK — more than OK. No matter what, Hashem is constantly, 24/7, providing me with the wherewithal to thrive.

THE BLESSING OF HASHEM'S POWERS

This blessing seems to be all about the revival of the dead. But, it is known as *Gevuros* — Hashem's power. Now, I appreciate that it's an impressive feat to take someone who has died and bring him back to life, but it is only one example of Hashem's powers. Why is it used so extensively in this blessing as, seemingly, the greatest expression of Hashem's power?

I used to see this blessing as talking about a very specific event that will happen sometime in the distant future. It sounded great, but it just didn't fit for me in the context of the first three blessings, whose purpose is about trying to create a feeling of connection. There are lots of prophecies and promises about the future, and the idea of the revival of the dead is for sure an uplifting and hopeful one. But there are lots of great events that we have been promised will take place in the future; why place a blessing about this one over here? Furthermore, as an example of Hashem's power it doesn't seem like the greatest nor the most tangible. In fact, the Gemara tells us that even the least of the Tanna'im could revive the dead.[83]

---

83. *Avodah Zarah* 10b

Chapter 4

Obviously, I cannot deny that according to the simple meaning of the blessing, it is talking about the future revival of the dead, and many of the commentaries explain it this way. However, I want to share another understanding that I learned from Rabbi Weinberg which has been incredibly helpful for me in terms of finding meaning and connection through this blessing.

Rabbi Weinberg said that this blessing is about Hashem being the Sustainer.

This is even more confusing. What has Hashem bringing everyone back to life at some point in the future got to do with Him sustaining the universe right now?

And then I put one and one together and it made two!

What do we mean when we say Hashem is the Sustainer? It means, in essence, that He did not create the universe and then walk away, not only in terms of intervening in the direction the universe goes (I will talk about this later, in the explanation for "Supervisor"), but also in terms of actively running the day-to-day mechanics of the universe.

It could not be any other way. The Infinite Being cannot create something independent of Him. If He could, there would be something that was not Him, and He would therefore not be infinite. Hashem cannot set a universe to run on its own because there is no power outside of Him to run anything. It would be akin to trying to make toast in a toaster that is not plugged in. Even though, superficially, it looks as though it runs on its own, if you take away its power source it will be unable to do so.

On a more philosophical level, our existence is dependent on His, just as my thoughts are dependent on me. If I close my eyes and imagine an elephant, it only exists as long as I continue to imagine it. The moment I stop imagining, the elephant ceases to exist. I don't have to destroy the elephant to get rid of it, I just have to think about something else instead and it is gone immediately. So too with us. In the morning service we say that Hashem is "*mechadesh b'chol yom maaseh bereishis'"* — He recreates the world every single day. That's what this means. Not just every day but every moment, He is creating the world by thinking about it, so to speak. Should Hashem stop thinking about His world, it would cease to exist at that very moment.

This is what we mean by "Sustainer." He is sustaining the very fabric of the universe's existence at every moment. He doesn't create the force of gravity, He *is* the force of gravity. He doesn't make strong and weak nuclear forces that hold atoms together, He *is* those forces. He didn't set the world up such that Planet Earth spins on its axis. *He* spins Earth 24/7, and were He to stop doing so, Earth would no longer spin — no matter what the laws of physics might suggest. In order to create the environment in which our free will can flourish, He acts consistently, and scientists call that consistency the "laws of nature." They are an illusion created to mask Hashem's direct involvement in our world so that we can choose to ignore Him (which makes our choices to embrace Him all the more meaningful).

Now, let's consider what reviving the dead might mean in this context.

In general, we think of ourselves as being alive, then we ask Hashem to help keep us that way. We pray, "Don't let us get sick," "Let us arrive safely at our destination," etc. Our perspective is that life is the status quo and it would take some sort of outside force to change that. And so we ask Hashem to protect us from such outside forces.

But, on consideration, that's not how it works. How does my heart beat? Hashem is actively beating it. How do my lungs breathe? Hashem is actively expanding and

Chapter 4

contracting them. How do I think? Hashem is actively sending me the thoughts to think. He is, in essence, thinking them for me.

The status quo is not that I am alive. The status quo is that I am dead. And Hashem, in His infinite mercy, continues making me alive (until, at some point, He no longer will). I am "dead," and Hashem is consciously reviving me. Right now. At every moment. He is, so to speak, "aliving" me. And if He were to stop doing so for even an instant, I would be dead immediately. It would not be that He killed me. It would be that He simply stopped "aliving" me, and so I reverted to my natural human state when Hashem does not intervene — dead.

So, it takes moment-to-moment conscious acts on Hashem's part to beat my heart, to breathe my lungs, to digest my food. Without that input, I would not die. I would just no longer be alive.

אַתָּה גִבּוֹר לְעוֹלָם ה׳. מְחַיֶּה מֵתִים אַתָּה רַב לְהוֹשִׁיעַ, **"You are powerful forever, Hashem; You cause the dead to be alive; You are great to provide salvation"**

Now, let's take a look at this wonderful blessing.

I am a lifeless body. If I am alive and conscious it is because You, Hashem, are — right this very moment and very actively — making me alive. You are here right now with me, aware of me, considering me, deciding to continue to give me life and actively doing so.

Suggestion:

This is something I do for myself that I find to be really helpful. I feel my pulse as I say these words and other similar ones in the blessing. As I feel my heart beating, I realize that Hashem is the beater. It's not happening on its own. It's almost like Hashem is speaking to me through my pulse. Every beat says to me: *I'm here... I'm here... I'm here... I'm here.* Nonstop for as long as I am alive, my heart beats *I'm here... I'm here... I'm here.*

Alternatively, I focus on my breathing. As my lungs expand and contract, I feel Hashem's very active involvement in my life. Or I simply allow myself to feel the tingling of my senses — in my hands, my arms, my legs... the tingling of Hashem's presence.

The opening blessing of *Shemoneh Esrei* was about Hashem's love. This one is about Hashem's presence — His continual, active engagement in my life.

"You settle the wind and bring down the rain" (said in the winter months from Shemini Atzeres until Pesach), מַשִּׁיב הָרוּחַ וּמוֹרִיד הַגֶּשֶׁם

This is another example of Hashem actively sustaining His creation. The wind does not blow, Hashem blows it. The rain does not fall, Hashem pushes down every single drop. This phrase is only said in the winter months because its power is in its tangibility. I stand saying *Shemoneh Esrei* as the wind howls outside. And as I say these words, I hear Hashem's presence in the wind. The wind is not howling, Hashem is howling, so to speak. As the rain clatters down around me, again, Hashem is in every raindrop. I close my eyes and imagine a million raindrops falling (in a reasonable rainstorm, that many drops will fall in a square mile in less than a second). I imagine Hashem pushing and guiding each one to the earth. They are not falling because of gravity. Gravity is just Hashem acting in a consistent way. Each and every raindrop only arrives on the ground because Hashem pushed it down every single step of the way. I imagine that as I stand listening to the rain, Hashem is here right now pushing down more than a million raindrops every second! Take a moment to reflect on that, to let the magnitude of Hashem's greatness. (That's why this blessing is called *Gevuros* — Hashem's "Power.")

To a lesser extent, this is true of the words *"morid hatal* — He brings down dew" (said in the summer months by those whose *nusach* includes it). I once watched a video of dew forming on a spider's web and a blade of grass. It was amazing to watch it happen and know that Hashem is actively making that process happen. I visualize this video in my mind when I say the words and again feel connected to Hashem's presence in the world.

"You מְכַלְכֵּל חַיִּים בְּחֶסֶד, SUSTAIN THE LIVING WITH KINDNESS"

Hashem provides us with all that we require to live, on an ongoing basis, giving us the sustenance that we need in order to remain alive: oxygen, water, warmth, food, shelter, protection — the list is a very long one. Hashem is continually providing it — not, as we discussed, that He set up the system and lets it run on its own.

"You are causing the dead to be alive with great mercy", מְחַיֶּה מֵתִים בְּרַחֲמִים רַבִּים

It is indeed mercy because no one would know the difference if He did it or not. If all of us ceased to exist, we would have no complaints — because we would not exist to be able to complain! Hence, it is with great mercy for us that He consistently breathes life into our dead bodies. There is no compelling reason for Hashem to do this other than out of a feeling of mercy for His children.

"You are supporting those falling", סוֹמֵךְ נוֹפְלִים

I am constantly falling because gravity is pulling me down 24/7. The only reason I remain upright is because Hashem is supporting me as I fall.

"You are healing the sick", רוֹפֵא חוֹלִים

My body is sick. It does not work on its own. It is full of bacteria and attacked by viruses at every moment.[84] The only reason I feel well is because Hashem is healing me moment to moment. It's not that He is *protecting* me from

---

84. A recent study by the Weizmann Institute found that the average human body is made up of around 30 trillion cells and is host to around 100 trillion bacteria cells. Many of them are incredibly helpful, such as viridans streptococci, which colonize the human throat. Some are helpful, but even those that are potentially dangerous are harmless, because Hashem is constantly "healing the sick" and ensuring that we are not negatively affected by them and their many "colleagues" that inhabit our bodies.

illness. He is healing the illness that is constantly surrounding me.⁸⁵

מַתִּיר אֲסוּרִים, "You are releasing the bound"

The Gemara says that the *yetzer hara* (evil inclination) of a human being gets stronger every day and seeks to "kill" him, and were it not for Hashem's assistance, he could not defeat it.⁸⁶ The illusory world that we live in is so attractive and enticing. Were it not for Hashem's assistance, we could not help but become hopelessly and forever bound in the chains of the evil inclination. As it is, we get stuck in so many ways. No one, especially with the enhanced distractions of our generation in the form of numerous digital devices with a multitude of content with which to engage, is entirely immune to the enticements and addictions that we are constantly faced with. And that's *with* Hashem's assistance. Without His constant and consistent "releasing of the bound," we would simply have no chance.

---

85. For example, in simple terms, the hydrochloric acid in the stomach, which is essential in order to break down and digest our food, is corrosive for the cells of the body. Hashem is, however, constantly "healing" us from this acid by lining the stomach with alkali, which protects it from the acid. Were Hashem not doing this for us, the acid in our body would simply eat through our stomach and then continue into the other organs. We would not last very long, killed by a substance that our body itself produced. Indeed, a peptic ulcer occurs when the stomach's membrane, for one reason or another, is compromised, and the stomach acid damages the stomach itself. Such ulcers cause as many as 6,500 deaths a year.
86. *Kiddushin* 30b.

וּמְקַיֵּם אֱמוּנָתוֹ לִישֵׁנֵי עָפָר,
"And You establish Your trustworthiness to the dust sleepers"

It does not say *b'afar*, which could imply that one sleeps "in" the dust. It merely says *liyesheinei afar*, literally, "dust sleepers." I would suggest that dust is an adjective describing the word "sleepers." In other words, we are sleepers made of dust. Dust is a collection of small particles. At the time that many of these ideas were translated, these tiny particles were the smallest ones known to man. However, nowadays, we know that there are molecules, atoms, and even smaller particles — things we can only see in an atomic microscope. I understand this to mean, then, that we human beings are "particle sleepers." We are unconscious beings put together from neutral atoms. There is very little to us in essence. As the verse in *Tehillim* says, "What is a man that You should even remember him?"[87] And yet, Hashem establishes His trustworthiness to us particle sleepers. We can trust Him. My heart will be beating in five minutes. I will continue to breathe while I sleep. I will wake up again tomorrow. I can trust Him to do all of those things. In spite of my incredible insignificance in the scheme of the universe, I can rely on Him to be here for me and provide me with continued and ongoing life.

---

87. *Tehillim* 8:4

— Chapter 4 —

מִי כָמוֹךָ בַּעַל גְּבוּרוֹת וּמִי דּוֹמֶה לָּךְ, "Who is like You, Master of powers, and who is similar to You?"

I have a little something that I do here. I think of the things that I want or need and I think of who might, in my mind, be able to give them to me. Let's take an easy one: money. Who could give me money? Well, this guy is a millionaire; this guy is a billionaire. If I needed money, surely they are the ones who could give it to me. But is this really true? Their money is here today, gone tomorrow. They themselves are here today, gone tomorrow. They are subject to changing moods. They might like me now and not like me in five minutes. There are so many variables. But Hashem? That's a different story. "Who is like You? Who is even similar?"

Let's say I am not well and need to be healed. Which doctor could help me? Pick the world's greatest. Can he help? What can he do? What does he know? Numerous times in my life, I have seen doctors reach the end of medical science and have no more solutions. But Hashem? "Who is like You? Who is even similar?"

מֶלֶךְ מֵמִית וּמְחַיֶּה, "King, Who kills and brings back to life"

I struggled with this phrase for many years. It was hard for me to see it as anything other than on a very practical level: Hashem takes us out of this world and then, at some point in the future, will bring us back.

And then I had a flash of inspiration.

Let me stress again: This is what I understand *Shemoneh Esrei* to be about. You try to understand what it means, you try again, you try again – then somewhere along the way, Hashem gives you a solution and it suddenly makes sense to you. And then it's yours forever. Once you have found your own relationship and your own understanding of the ideas — one that really speaks to you — you will be able to use *Shemoneh Esrei* to give you the connection that is its purpose. Of course, this is a lifelong process, and as long as you are looking to continually improve your understanding, there are deeper and deeper levels to be had.

So, what does it mean to me that Hashem "kills"? I realize that it's a harsh statement in the context of what we have said until now. It's all been about Hashem's love, Hashem's kindness, Hashem's mercy and His trustworthiness. Now, all of a sudden, we are praising Hashem because He kills?

So here's how I see it.

I think there is no human being in this world that does not fear death on some level. It's a frightening concept as it is ultimately so unknown to us.

Even for someone who believes in Hashem, the thought of death has the power to strike fear in the human heart.

The fear of death takes many forms: *What if I am in a terror attack? What if the plane I'm on crashes? What if I have a heart attack or an aneurysm? What if I am diagnosed with cancer? What if, what if, what if?* The modes of death are endless, but the fear is always the same.

How comforting, how incredibly comforting it is for me to know that *Hashem* kills!

I cannot be hit by a bus and die. Hashem can decide it is time for me to go and send a bus to kill me. There is no *random* cardiac arrest. Hashem simply decides that my time is over in this world and actively and consciously stops my heart from beating. There are no accidents. I can't die while Hashem is distracted by something else! No. The only killer in the world is Hashem Himself. And so, He will be right there with me when I die.

My time will come in this world — that I can say with absolute certainty. But as I say these words in *Shemoneh Esrei*, I remember that I can say with equal certainty that the moment of my death will be an incredibly intimate one. Hashem will be right with me all the way, no matter how it might happen. And so, I have nothing to fear.

This one touches me to no end, because it converts my insecurities into something deep and comforting.

But there is more. Not only does He kill, but He also gives us life again. In other words, death is not an end. He kills — but even as part of that killing, He is giving us life again. The soul lives on after we die. Although even our greatest Sages have said that they do not know how that will look, death will not be the end for us. And that's reassuring to know!

וּמַצְמִיחַ יְשׁוּעָה, "And sprouts forth redemption"

Redemption is an active and continual process. In every difficult and painful situation, redemption is already inherent and developing. As the Gemara tells us, Hashem creates the cure before He creates the illness.[88] No matter how difficult a situation a person is in, nothing new needs to happen from Hashem's perspective. The seeds of change

---

88. *Megillah* 13b

are not just already planted, they are already growing. A person just needs to find those flourishing seeds and from them find a solution.

וְנֶאֱמָן אַתָּה לְהַחֲיוֹת מֵתִים.
בָּרוּךְ אַתָּה ה' מְחַיֵּה הַמֵּתִים,
"YOU ARE TRUSTWORTHY TO GIVE LIFE TO THE DEAD. YOU ARE A WELLSPRING OF GOODNESS, HASHEM, WHO GIVES LIFE TO THE DEAD"

A reminder that we can rely absolutely on Hashem to continue giving us life (even if not in this world, certainly continued life in the next). It's very much on His agenda.

Practical suggestion

At this point in *Shemoneh Esrei* I think of people whom Hashem will be reuniting me with at a later date. I picture my late wife and my father. And I think of the fact that in His infinite kindness to me, He will give them back to me. I will see them again. Not only that, but a time will come when I will be on such a list for my loved ones who will outlive me. And that's OK too. Hashem will give them back to me too when their lives are over, and I can rest assured that Hashem's love is such that my loved ones and I will be together for eternity — that's the type of God I am talking to and connecting to. I feel a deep sense of gratitude and hence connection when I consider this.

— CHAPTER 4 —

THE BLESSING OF HASHEM'S HOLINESS

The next blessing is, as mentioned above, about Hashem as "Supervisor." Hashem not only created our world with love and continues to sustain it moment to moment, He also supervises our lives. He has a goal for us and a plan for how that will happen. He is aware of us, guiding us and directing us constantly, and updating the plan as we change routes.

This means that our lives are meaningful. What we do matters. "Eat, drink, and be merry for tomorrow you will die" could not be further from the truth. "Use your time productively and effectively for tomorrow you will die" is much more the Jewish perspective.

One third of the words that make up the body of this blessing have the root *kadosh*. The basic definition of this root is "holy." Taking this a step further, my understanding of this root is "meaningful." Hashem was *mekadesh es haShabbos* — He gave the day meaning such that people could defer activity and return to relationship; it was set aside for something meaningful. He was also *mekadesh* the Jewish people — He gave us the meaning of being a nation of priests who would teach other nations about Hashem. He gave us a meaningful goal and set us apart so that we could achieve it.

So now on to the blessing.

אַתָּה קָדוֹשׁ, "YOU ARE HOLY"

Whereas Hashem was *mekadesh* Shabbos and the Jewish people — He made them holy — He did not make Himself holy. He simply *is* holy. He is meaning itself. He is the essence of holiness. All other things are made holy by Hashem. Hashem Himself, however, is holy simply because He *is* holy. He is the source of meaning; He is only meaning.

וְשִׁמְךָ קָדוֹשׁ, "And Your Name is holy"

A name is a word through which we relate to another person. The person is not his name, but we associate his name with our own perception of him. So too, when we talk about Hashem's Name, we mean Hashem as He is manifest in this world, not Hashem in His true nature. We do not see Hashem in this world, we see a manifestation of Hashem, or a reflection of Hashem. It is as if we see Hashem's shadow. A shadow is a two-dimensional, colorless image of a three-dimensional, colorful object. It's a poor representation, but it gives us an idea of what it is.

The blessing is now saying that even this limited way, so to speak, that we are able to perceive Hashem in this world is incredibly meaningful.

But more than that . . .

Chapter 4

וּקְדוֹשִׁים בְּכָל יוֹם יְהַלְלוּךָ סֶּלָה, בָּרוּךְ אַתָּה ה' הָאֵ-ל הַקָּדוֹשׁ "**AND HOLY BEINGS PRAISE YOU EVERY DAY. YOU ARE A WELLSPRING OF BLESSING, HASHEM, ALMIGHTY, THE ONLY SOURCE OF MEANING.**"

That's what beings who are themselves holy do — they ascribe and attribute their holiness to Hashem. There is simply nothing, in either the physical or spiritual universe, that is in any way holy that does not owe its holiness directly to Hashem.

Hashem, our Creator and Sustainer, is also the source of all meaning. Hence, our lives matter. We matter. Hashem ensures that that is the case.

The Middle Blessings of Request

The middle blessings really deserve a book unto themselves. Not only are there thirteen in a regular weekday *Shemoneh Esrei*, but those thirteen become a single, yet different, blessing for each of the four Shabbos *Shemoneh Esreis* as well as for Yom Tov, Rosh Chodesh, Rosh HaShanah, and Yom Kippur. In all, there would be twenty-one different blessings to explain. However, since I want to keep this book as short and simple as possible as a first book on prayer and leave certain elements for another time, I will instead discuss personalizing the middle blessings to make them your own, as well as include explanations of their meaning in my conceptual translations at the end.

Personalizing

The *Shulchan Aruch* devotes a whole section to the idea of personalizing the middle blessings.[89] It says that "whoever wishes to add his own personal prayers into each of the middle blessings, that is related to each blessing, should do so."

The *Sefer Chassidism* goes further and says that one should "add into each blessing according to your own needs . . . and if you cannot add into each blessing, then at least add into one or two."[90]

The Shelah says that one should "add requests and wishes in some of the blessings of *Shemoneh Esrei* if not in all of them."[91] He brings this as one of the ten ways to have *kavanah* in prayer.

The *Shulchan Aruch* clarifies that this is not talking about the first three or last three blessings as they are not requests at all, rather, as I have explained, praises and thanks, and should not be added to.[92]

Based on this, if you know someone who is sick and you are praying for him, you should add your personal prayers for him in *Refa'einu*, the Blessing of Health. If you are struggling financially and need assistance, you should add your personal prayers into the blessing of *Barech Aleinu*, the Blessing of Sustenance. The place to add it in each blessing is right before the closing of the blessing, before one says *baruch Attah*.

We are not talking here about the standardized format that you will find in many siddurim. That is simply an additional form and not personalization. Instead, when we

---

89. *Orach Chaim* 119
90. *Sefer Chassidim* 158
91. *Tamid, Ner Mitzvah* 13
92. *Orach Chaim* 112

get to the blessing itself, we should stop and add our own prayer in the language we are most comfortable.

Rabbi Weinberg once told me that he heard from Dayan Yechezkel Abramsky that he was once praying next to the Chofetz Chaim and heard him speaking Yiddish in the middle of his *Shemoneh Esrei*. Dayan Abramsky was surprised and asked what was going on. The Chofetz Chaim answered that he was adding his own personal prayers in the middle of the blessings. Knowing the Chofetz Chaim to be fluent in Hebrew, Dayan Abramsky asked him why he would pray in Yiddish and not Hebrew. The Chofetz Chaim answered that "*mamme lashon* (one's mother tongue) is better!" Obviously, this does not mean that the Chofetz Chaim prayed *Shemoneh Esrei* itself in Yiddish. It means that when he added in his own personal prayers, he did so in Yiddish.

I see no advantage to praying these personal requests of *Shemoneh Esrei* in Hebrew if it is not your first language. The purpose of these personal prayers is precisely that — to make your *Shemoneh Esrei* personal, something that is from your heart, something that can perhaps be "calling out to Hashem in sincerity." The only way to express oneself in a way that is intimate and personal is in the language one is most comfortable and intimate with, whatever it may be.

As an interesting suggestion, the Shelah says that if it is at all practical, a person should accustom himself to speak in Hebrew with family and friends so that he would be able to both pray in Hebrew and do so with meaning.[93] While the Shelah is, of course talking about *Lashon HaKodesh*, fluency in modern Hebrew would clearly make someone more comfortable with the language of prayer.

---

93. Ibid. 15

Suggestion

Let me talk for a moment about things that a person might want to add and which blessings they might fit into. The obvious ones I have already mentioned, but let me suggest a few more. Although the Rabbis say that one can add any request he wants into *Shema Koleinu* at the end, I find it much more meaningful to add each request in its appropriate blessing so that the blessing itself takes on more meaning. Also, if one is "saving" all his personal prayers for *Shema Koleinu*, it can mean that most of *Shemoneh Esrei* is said without any personal element, which is crammed in at the end. As the Rishonim and Acharonim quoted above have suggested, there is great advantage to adding each element in its appropriate place.

So, let's look at some things one might be inclined to pray for.

אַתָּה חוֹנֵן — Blessing of Understanding

Requests to pass an exam would be included in the first blessing, the blessing for knowledge, as would a prayer to help us understand a message that Hashem is sending us, to understand something in His Torah, or to give us insight if we are struggling to figure out what is best for one of our children.

הֲשִׁיבֵנוּ — Blessing of Repentance

If we are struggling to change something in ourselves, the second of these blessings is the appropriate place to ask for assistance. This blessing is about requests for spiritual change. If we always get up late and want help to change that, we know we should apologize to someone but can't get ourselves to do so, or we want to improve in any other way, we can insert a request here.

סְלַח לָנוּ — Blessing of Forgiveness

In the previous blessing, we asked for *teshuvah* — spiritual change. But even when we change and fix our mistakes, there is a residual feeling of disappointment for what we have done. For this, we need forgiveness if we are to be able to move forward in life with our self-respect and dignity intact.

There is no one in this world who does not make mistakes. That privilege is left to Hashem alone. As *Koheles* tells us, "When it comes to human beings, there is no righteous person on earth who does good and does not transgress."[94] Making mistakes and seeking forgiveness is part of life. Hashem, Who, as this blessing says, "pardons and forgives," will always forgive. The key question is whether we are able to forgive ourselves. The feeling of disappointment and frustration that we are not using our potential, wasting our time, and damaging the pure soul that Hashem's love bestowed upon us — that feeling is what we ask Hashem to assuage. Hashem will forgive us, but we also ask Him to help us forgive ourselves.

---

94. *Koheles* 7:20

רְאֵה בְעָנְיֵנוּ — Blessing of Redemption

If you look at the structure of the thirteen requests that form the middle blessings of the weekday *Shemoneh Esrei*, you will see that they start with personal requests and move on to national requests. So a request for redemption (which we normally associate with the coming of Moshiach) seems out of place here, especially given the fact that we ask much more explicitly for Moshiach later on. Clearly, this blessing is talking about personal redemption. I see this as the times in life when we are completely stuck and see no way out. It might be physical — stuck in a prison cell and the key has been thrown away, or, more likely, it might be spiritual — addicted to something that we have been doing for years, caught in a terrible relationship that we see no way of repairing . . . This is the place to pray for redemption, because Hashem is the only possible solution.

רְפָאֵנוּ — Blessing of Health

I feel that this is more than just a prayer for health. Anything to do with the physical body or broader health issues — for example, even if one is training for a marathon and wants to become strong and healthy — can be inserted here. Whether one is on a diet and looking to lose weight or is praying for a healthy pregnancy, an easy labor, and a healthy baby, these would fit into the blessing of *Refa'einu*. The Rabbis tell us that the prayers of the sick person himself are listened to more than those of others who pray for him,[95] so, yes, pray for others — but make sure you also pray for yourself!

בָּרֵךְ עָלֵינוּ — Blessing of Sustenance

In the blessing of *Barech Aleinu*, which deals with financial blessings, we can add more than a request to just make ends meet. This prayer is for all of our material needs. If you are looking to buy a new house and want to ask to find the right one, if you need a job or you have a friend who needs a job, if your car broke down and needs fixing sooner rather than later . . . all this fits in here. (Remember, nothing is too small to pray for. Quite the opposite, by praying for the small things, we remind ourselves that Hashem controls *everything* in the world, not just the big things.)

תְּקַע בְּשׁוֹפָר — Blessing of the Ingathering of the Jewish People

In this blessing, I often try to think of Jews I know, and feel close to, who are distant from Eretz Yisrael, and I pray that they be gathered back there along with myself and everyone else. But more powerfully, at least for me, I think of Jews I know who are distant from the Jewish people — disconnected, disaffiliated, disinterested, perhaps married out of the Jewish faith. I speak to Hashem, saying that they are good people, they are Jewish souls, His children, who are innocently lost and distant from Him and His Torah,

---

95. *Rashi, Shemos* 21:17

and I ask that He bring them back to a relationship with Him and with the Jewish people. As usual, the more specific you can be with specific people that you know, the more likely you are to pray with meaning.

הָשִׁיבָה שׁוֹפְטֵינוּ — BLESSING OF JUSTICE

We do not live in a "fair" world. People live righteous lives and are taken advantage of and abused with no one to protect them. And those who take advantage of others often get away with it. There was a time when, while not perfect, we had a system in place to implement and enforce laws that were just and fair. We are praying for a return for this. Thinking of the injustices you see around you and in the world and the suffering people go through as a result, and then asking for justice to be returned so that things can change, can go a long way in improving your *kavanah* in this blessing.

וְלַמַּלְשִׁינִים — BLESSING OF THE DEFEAT OF OUR ENEMIES

Unfortunately, as a nation, we have had many enemies over the years and we have suffered greatly. While we don't ask that our enemies die, we do ask that they be rendered powerless to harm us. We also ask that the "evil" be destroyed, not "evil people" — a big difference. Ultimately, the final word of the blessing asks that they be "humbled." And, hopefully, from that humility, they will find their way back to Hashem, Who will embrace them.

Chapter 4

עַל הַצַּדִּיקִים — Blessing of Reward for the Righteous

This blessing ends with "let us not feel ashamed . . ." We are children of Avraham, Yitzchak, and Yaakov. We have a spiritual heritage like no other. But what have we done with our lives? What legacy will we leave? What mark will we make on Jewish history? We ask in this blessing that we should live lives that will give us a seat at the table of Jewish history, that we should be able to look back on our lives with heads held high.

וְלִירוּשָׁלַיִם עִירְךָ — Blessing of the Rebuilding of Jerusalem

Although Jerusalem is indeed rebuilt, the rebuilding we are asking for is far from complete. We ask for a Jerusalem that is a spiritual city, a beacon of light that shines forth to the world, "for out of Zion shall go forth Hashem's Torah."[96] Jerusalem is not that spiritual city today — far from it. We pray that one day soon, it will be.

אֶת צֶמַח דָּוִד עַבְדְּךָ מְהֵרָה תַצְמִיחַ — Blessing of the Messianic Era

This is the request for the Messianic era. Think of the suffering in the world that would not be here if the world knew about Hashem, the suffering of our exile. Surely two

---

96. *Yeshayah* 2:3

thousand years are enough, Hashem? Specifically, I always think of hatred and war, of the intense suffering that people go through with mental illness, of the lost and distant Jews who have no relationship with Judaism. There's plenty to add to that list, and the more tangible you can make it for yourself, the more you will be able to ask Hashem sincerely that He change things.

שְׁמַע קוֹלֵנוּ — Blessing That Our Prayers Be Answered

As I said earlier, on the one hand, this is a general and generic prayer in which you can add any request that you have not fitted into the previous blessings. However, there is also a specific request in this prayer — that Hashem listens to our prayers. We are asking Hashem to take us seriously, to listen to what we say and respond. It's interesting to note that it says "*shema koleinu* — listen to our voices," not "listen to our words" or "to our prayers." It comes back to the theme that Hashem hears the feeling behind the prayer, "the voice" more so than the words. "Hashem wants the heart."[97] "Hashem listens . . . to all who call to Him in truth."[98] This is the essence of prayer, and if we can get our "voice" right, then Hashem will surely listen and respond.

In Conclusion

In general, it goes without saying that the way one personalizes these blessings is according to the modes of

---

97. *Sanhedrin* 106b
98. *Tehillim* 145:18

prayer mentioned above. It's not just a matter of running through a list of generic needs or throwing in the name of a sick person, although that would be better than nothing. It is a matter of standing before Hashem and praying to Him with all of our heart. If you think that doing this might make your *Shemoneh Esrei* extremely long, you are correct. Remember, every moment spent in prayer is invaluable. In fact, the early pious ones that I have mentioned before used to spend an hour praying every *Shemoneh Esrei*.

The Three Blessings of Thanks

This leaves us with the last three blessings of thanks.

As with the blessings of request, I will say some general thoughts about them, but, once again, I wish to include a more detailed explanation in a later book.

Why do we thank Hashem at the end of *Shemoneh Esrei*?

We have just spent thirteen blessings pouring our hearts out, telling Hashem what we don't have and feeling the pain of not having it. We don't want to leave it at that. We want to remember that, in spite of all that we do not have and are praying for, life is great just the way that it is. We are so blessed and so fortunate to be alive in this wonderful and beautiful world which Hashem has created for us. We thank Hashem after we have made our requests to remember this and leave *Shemoneh Esrei* with a feeling of gratitude, not one of lacking.

Let me share a thought on each of the three blessings of thanks.

רְצֵה — Blessing of the Divine Service

At first glance, this blessing does not look like it is thanking Hashem at all. It is in the format of another request. One explanation is that we are asking in this blessing for Hashem to return the Divine service to the Beis HaMikdash so that we may serve Him. In essence, we are saying that we cannot properly express thanksgiving without a Beis HaMikdash. We recognize this before we say our thanks, and then we ask that we be allowed to thank Hashem in the proper and appropriate manner in the future. Then we go into the next blessing — which is clearly one of thanks — and do the best we can to thank Him in spite of our lacking the ultimate means of doing so.

מוֹדִים אֲנַחְנוּ לָךְ — Blessing of Thanks

This is the main blessing of thanks in *Shemoneh Esrei*. We thank Hashem for our lives, both of the physical body and of the Godly soul with which we are endowed. We thank Him for the ongoing miracles that we see each day. Whether we notice it or not, our heart beating and our lungs breathing are moment-to-moment miracles that are with us until the day that we die. This blessing is also a great opportunity to take a moment and thank Hashem for any previous prayers that He has answered.

שִׂים שָׁלוֹם — Blessing of Peace

As with the Blessing of the Divine Service, at first glance, this does not look like a blessing of thanks; it seems to be another request. I have heard it said that this blessing is actually connected to the Priestly blessing that precedes it (and ends with a request for peace) and is not per se a blessing of thanksgiving, but this is difficult to understand since it does not fit with what the Rambam says in *Hilchos Tefillah*.[99] Another explanation is that in asking for "peace," we are not requesting the superficial peace of this world — peace with other human beings. Rather, we are requesting spiritual peace — being at peace with ourselves, that the battle between the evil inclination and the good inclination be over and that our bodies and souls desire to serve Hashem. Similar to the Blessing of the Divine Service, we ask that Hashem put us into a position whereby the main impediment to gratitude, namely, the ego, is gone and we can express our thanks in the fullest and deepest way possible.

---

99. *Rambam Hilchos Tefillah* 1:4

Conclusion for the Reader

I hope that this book will ultimately improve your sense of connection with Hashem as you pray. As I said in my introduction, the Shelah refers to two groups of people, the former being those who do what they do with meaning and understanding, in particular *davening*. It is my own prayer for you, dear reader, who has made the effort to journey with me all the way to the end of my book, that you will always be a member of this former group and continue to find the joy, uplift, inspiration, and ultimately, the blessing that genuine and heartfelt *tefillah* brings.

If there is interest in a follow-up book that talks in more detail about the other brachos in the Shemoneh Esrei, as well as those in the Shabbos and Festival Shemoneh Esrei also, I will gladly write one. Please email me at meanwhatyoupray@tikun.co.uk and if I receive ten responses, I will be happy to write part two.

Appendix

Conceptual Shemoneh Esrei

This "conceptual translation" of the Shabbos *Shemoneh Esrei* is primarily for readers who have little or no relationship with Hebrew, *Shemoneh Esrei*, or its concepts. My goal is that rather than pray nothing, they should pray something that is relatable for them that sticks to the essence of the ideas of *Shemoneh Esrei* itself. I am *not* suggesting that a person who would otherwise pray *Shemoneh Esrei* in Hebrew or say the direct English translation should substitute this prayer instead. It is for someone who does not relate to *Shemoneh Esrei* and hence does not pray it.

However, even people who do pray *Shemoneh Esrei* regularly can gain from this "conceptual translation" as it gives a sense of the flow and conceptual direction that the *Shemoneh Esrei* is taking us in, which can help one to pray his own *Shemoneh Esrei* with more meaning.

Almighty Father Who created this whole universe, time, space, and matter, You love us with a love that is beyond the love of any parent for his child. Your love has been a love of 5,782 years and counting and is not dependent on our actions. You love us because of who we are, not what we do. Every human being makes mistakes and, like a good parent, You don't condemn us for our mistakes, You support us through them. You are a helper when we are struggling, a savior when we have real problems, and a shield to ensure that problems do not arise. You are the source of all goodness, Hashem, shield of Avraham.

You have the power to do anything. You constantly breathe life into the dead flesh that is our bodies. You are the force that holds together every molecule in this universe. You can bring the dead back to life as easily as You can sustain the living. You have the cure for all illness. You have the key to every prison. You can alleviate any of our suffering — be it physical, emotional, or spiritual. You, and only You, have the solution to any and all of our problems. No one and nothing else is even similar in their ability. You are the source of all goodness, Hashem, Who holds our physical bodies together.

You know our every emotion. You know our worries, our concerns, our fears, our problems. You know them better than we do. Nothing is hidden from You. You respond to us and relate to us. Every occurrence in this world is meaningful. Nothing is random, nothing chance. You are the source of all goodness, Hashem, the essence of meaning.

You made the seventh day into a day of meaning, the purpose of all of creation. Deeper blessing is available to us on this day than on mundane weekdays. A deeper feeling of spiritual connection is inherent within this time. And this idea is talked about in Your Torah, as it says:

"And the spiritual and physical worlds coalesced into form. And Hashem completed, during the seventh phase of creation, His crafting of the Divine illusion. And Hashem ceased, during the seventh phase of creation, shaping the world of form. And Hashem blessed the seventh day and imbued holiness within the structure of its time. Because it was in this seventh phase that Hashem ceased from His active engagement in forming the Divine illusion."

Hashem, Who has loved our people for hundreds of generations, make our rest a rest of focus and meaning, not escape. May it be that we act in a way that lifts us up into You — please help us to do so. May Your commands assist us in coming close to You and not become empty and meaningless rituals. May we have a personal understanding of what this world is about and why we are here. May we take pleasure in Your abundant blessing and not be caught in always wanting more. Please blunt the desires that distract us from being who we really want to be. And may all of our desires and our emotions be focused only on being Godly and spiritual beings. You are the source of all goodness, Hashem, Who gives us Shabbos as an opportunity for meaning and inner focus.

Thank You for creating us in order to serve You. Please, once again, give us the opportunity to serve You in Jerusalem and show You how thankful we are for Your goodness. You are the source of all goodness, Hashem, Who returns his presence to Zion.

We bow before You, Father, Who has given us so much goodness. You have given us life itself. You have given us independence and free will. You have given us minds, bodies, emotions. Our lives are so rich, so full, so bountiful. And the world we live in is so abundant. We cannot thank You enough for all that You have done and continue to do for us in our day-to-day lives — every second of every minute of every hour of every day of our whole life, You are giving goodness, taking care of us, loving us, and looking after us.

Thank You Hashem for all of Your goodness. You are the source of all goodness, Hashem, Whose Name symbolizes goodness, and to You it is wonderful to be thankful.

You are constantly supervising our lives. Everything is meaningful. Thank You for believing in us always and constantly guiding us along a road that will ultimately lead us to perfect ourselves and being able to relate to You in a full and complete way. You are the source of all goodness, Hashem, Who constantly blesses His people, Israel, with the opportunity for perfection.

Glossary

Anshei Knesses HaGedolah — The Men of the Great Assembly
Avos — lit. fathers; Patriarchs
Avodah — Service
Beis HaMikdash — Holy Temple
brachah/brachos — blessing/blessings
Chessed — kindness
Emes — truth
Emunah — faith
Eretz Yisrael — Israel
halachah/halachos — laws
Hilchos — laws of
Kavanah — intention
Milchamah — war
Mitzvos — commandments
Moshiach — Messiah
Naakah —sighing in desperation
Nipul —throwing oneself down

— APPENDIX —

nusach — version of the prayers

Rinah — joy

Shemoneh Esrei — the main part of a prayer, comprised of nineteen blessings and recited while standing

Shul — synagogue

Sichah — conversation

Tachnunim — begging

Tefillah — prayer

Teshuvah — repentance

Tzaakah — crying out in desperation

Yam Suf — Sea of Reeds

Zechus — merit